TIEN MING

AN OUTLINE HISTORY
OF
CHINA

PART II

FROM THE MANCHU CONQUEST TO THE
RECOGNITION OF THE REPUBLIC
A. D. 1913

BY

HERBERT H. GOWEN, D.D., F.R.G.S.
Lecturer on Oriental History at the University
of Washington

BOSTON
SHERMAN, FRENCH & COMPANY
1913

PREFACE

In view of the kindly reception the first volume
of this "Outline History" has had at the hands
of the press and public, the author is hopeful that
the completion of the work will be as generously
judged. It still, however, seems necessary to
emphasize the fact that the book is neither a complete history of China nor a selection of episodes
chosen according to the writer's taste. The word
"Outline" is intended to be taken literally. The
bulk of the book might all too easily have been
increased, but in that event the idea of writing a
brief, fairly-proportioned sketch would have remained unfulfilled. One or two critics have com-
plained of the prominence of military episodes.
The only excuse that need be made is that (as the
Vicomte D'Ollone has so often repeated) Chinese
history is unfortunately very full of campaigns
which cannot be left unchronicled if a true picture is to be presented. At the same time the
Kulturgeschichte has by no means been neglected.
The philosophers and literati undoubtedly con-
tributed much to Chinese history. Nevertheless,
the framework of the story must necessarily be
political and the effect of such a work as the
present would have been invertebrate had not the

PREFACE

dynastic changes been carefully observed. The author believes that those who take the trouble to make this general outline their own will appreciate as they have not done before the ample materials provided elsewhere for filling up the gaps which have been deliberately left.

CONTENTS

ILLUSTRATIONS

CHAPTER I

INTRODUCTORY

A celebrated Japanese gardener, the story goes, set out to make a garden in which he should use but one of the manifold products of a bounteous earth. He chose, of all things in the world,—rocks! and we are told that his rock-garden was one of the wonders of the neighborhood. There are many who suppose that Chinese history must necessarily be, if a garden at all with any ordered plan, a garden of rocks, mere facts petrified with age, arranged according to the *preciosité* of some antiquarian or archæological schematism, but out of all relation with the things that live.

It is hoped that those who have hitherto followed this little history will have discovered that such an estimate is untrue. The forces which rule in modern China are not for the most part forces which have been imported from foreign lands. They are forces which come potent and alive out of the historic past.

A Chinese legend tells how in the fifth century B. C. a certain prince offended his sovereign and was ordered to commit suicide. The culprit obeyed and his body was cast into the great river

Yangtsze as he had requested. But he predicted that he would come again to behold the ruin of his ruthless master and the legend tells us that the great bore of Hangchow rolling seaward with "a wrathful sound, and the swift rush of thunder" is nothing else but the spirit of the unappeased Tsz-sü. In like manner the spirits of the past ages make to-day's tides. The spirit of the Revolution of 1912 was the same as that which swept away the Shang Dynasty eleven centuries before Christ, or that which drove back the Mongol into Central Asia in 1368 A. D. The democratic forces which have prevailed to-day are essentially the same as those which called Shun from his plowing twenty-five centuries before Christ, or made it possible for an obscure Buddhist priest to found the dynasty of the Mings.

All history, however modern, must take account of origins. The Knickerbocker history, which must needs go back to the patriarchs to commence the history of New York, is not wrong in principle. Not only is it true, as Shelley sings, that

> "All things, by a law divine,
> With one another's being mingle,"

but it is also true that the particular must always take hold of the universal. The drinking cup of every man, as well as that of Thor, is connected with the infinite ocean. He who would drain to the bottom his own draught must exhaust the sea.

All this is true of the history of China as well as that of any other country. The facts of China's past contain not only the interpretation of China's present: they contain also the interpretation of the history of Europe and America. As in Darwin's famous illustration the white clover disappeared from a certain district in Australia because the boys had killed off the cats which had hitherto destroyed the mice, now enabled to multiply and so destroy the nests of the bumble bees which had fertilized the clover, in history there is no scientific frontier between nations. Modern Europe rose on the ruins of the Roman Empire, which fell largely before the inroads of the barbarian tribes which the great Han generals of China had succeeded in turning westward; and modern America is the result of the dreams which Marco Polo inspired in the navigators of the fifteenth century of a Cathay rich and splendid beyond the imagination of mortal men.

All this needs to be emphasized because it would be a pity to attempt the understanding of China out of a study restricted to modern times. We need some far-flung vision of the past, with all its mist and all its glamor, if we would appreciate the present, which seems more prosaic because seen at closer range. To know a river in such a way as to account for its size, its currents, its swiftness, its color, the character of the soil brought down as a deposit for the fields on either hand, you must do more than stand upon its bank at a given point: you must search, if you can, "the roots of the fountain" and track it onwards to the ocean. Happy indeed if, while in other historic studies we see

> "In outline dim and vast
>   Their fearful shadows cast
> The giant forms of Empires, on their way
>   To ruin,"

we find in the case of China a commonwealth of unknown antiquity continually resisting the forces of disintegration, and a contemporary of the youngest as it was a contemporary of the most ancient nationalities the world has known. A French writer has recently said: *"Il n'est point si facile de faire table rase du vieux monde celeste."* The phrase is an apt one and applies with as much force to the revolution brought about by the Manchus in 1644 as to that which took place before our astonished eyes a year or two ago. There is no *table rase* at the commencement of the period with which this volume deals, and we must, therefore, bring to the study of the time some conception of the various epochs which gave it birth.

Let us bring with us to the study of the China of the past three centuries the following vision:

In the youth of the world, beyond the beginnings of authentic history, we see a shepherd folk in the northwest provinces of what we now call China, of whose provenance we can only speak by way of speculation.   These folk have learned to rule and guard and feed their sheep, and they bring to the ruling and guarding of the future Empire the self-same qualities which have made them shepherds.   Presently, the great family under its *"Pastores"* is seen to be outgrowing the old patriarchal despotism.   The machinery of a more complex government is being evolved, not only to secure the people from attacks from the fierce aboriginal tribes within their borders and to repel the hordes of invaders from without, but also to avert or heal the great devastations of flood and drought to which China has been subject for uncounted ages.

So we come to the dynastic history which, as given us in the later compilations of the Confucian literati, represents the monarchs of China in the strongest conceivable light and shade.   Like the little girl in the rhyme,

"When they were good they were very, very good,
    And when they were bad they were horrid."

There is some sameness in the story of these dynasties, for as Byron writes,—

"There is the moral of all human tales;
    'Tis but the same rehearsal of the past;
    First Freedom, and then Glory—when that fails,
    Wealth, Vice, Corruption—Barbarism at last.
    And History with all her volumes vast,
    Hath but one page."

With some such reflection we pass by the story of the vicissitudes of the dynasties of Hia and Shang to the nine centuries during which ruled the house of Chow. This we think of as the feudal period, when the centrifugal tendencies of the several states were stronger than the forces which were centripetal. It is during this period that we perceive philosophers and professional reformers of every type endeavoring to repair by ethical teaching the moral declension of the rulers. It is the era of Laotsz and Confucius, of Chwangtsz and of Mencius, of Micius and Licius. Nevertheless, all the philosophers with their democratic theories were not able to arrest a brief experiment in Imperialism, and for one generation, from about B. C. 250, we see the mighty fashioner of the Great Wall, Tsin Shih Hwang-ti, bending himself to the double task of rooting out from China the very memory of Confucian ideals and of welding together the contending principalities into an indissoluble unity. Tsin Shih Hwang-ti's dynasty perished with him, but that which followed, while reacting from the iconoclasm of the anti-Confucianists, carried out the great First Emperor's dream of extended rule and pushed on the frontiers of China to regions no ruler had hitherto known. The story of the Han dynasty and of those great Wardens of the Marches who reared the dragon flag front to front with the eagles of Rome on the one frontier which divided the Empire of the Pacific from that of the

Atlantic,—is one of thrilling historical and political interest. No one will ever quite understand the significance, *e. g.*, of the Russian Convention with Mongolia in 1912 who has not appreciated what the great Han generals accomplished two thousand years before.

Then there rises before us four centuries of anarchy, which have become for us centuries of romance, and we scarcely need the *"Story of the Three Kingdoms"* by China's Sir Walter Scott to make us feel the fascination of this rude yet chivalrous time. At the beginning of the 7th Century A. D., when from Japan to the Atlantic Coast new nations were rising into manhood, when on the ruins of the Roman Empire in the west a modern Europe was slowly taking shape, and on the ruins of the Byzantine Empire and of Sassanian Persia the Khalifate was establishing itself; when the *Nihongi* and *Kojiki* in Japan were telling of a new power rising from the mists of the eastern archipelago—rises into view the glorious period of the T'angs, memorable alike for its literature and its art, and above all, for the great religious movements which turned the China of the 7th Century into the hospitable nursing-mother of foreign religions, Magian, Muhamadan, Christian and Manichæan.

Once again we have a period of anarchy and misrule, and this in A. D. 960 gives place to the Sungs with their philosophers and political economists striving to hold back from ruin a land already to a large extent under the grip of the Tatar.

A mist of blood passes before the eyes through which sweeps westward with flashing sword the terrible form of Jenghiz Khan. When the storm had passed we see rising out of the ruins the throne of the Mongol. The fair city of Cambaluc gleams from afar like Camelot and through the magic spectacles of Marco Polo we catch a glimpse of Kublai Khan. We see him "with ten thousand falconers and some five hundred gerfalcons, besides peregrines, sakers and other hawks in great numbers; and goshawks also to fly at the waterfowl. The Emperor himself is carried upon four elephants in a fine chamber made of timber, lined inside with plates of beaten gold, and outside with lions' skins."

A century more and the Mongol rule has passed to the limbo to which it had itself consigned the Sungs. Out of the factions of the mid-fourteenth century rises the figure of the "Beggar King," achieving Empire almost without knowing whither his stars were leading him, and so founding the famous dynasty of the Mings.

Now at last our vision is almost finished. The Ming dynasty has, like its predecessors, sunk into the mire of contempt. The Manchus are thundering at the northern portals, but it is to rebellion and intrigue that the China of the Mings succumbs. The last Ming Emperor stands in the San Kwan temple close to the city gates to learn his fate. The fortune-telling sticks are in the vessel in his hand. If a long stick is shaken out he will go forth to meet the rebels; if a medium-sized stick falls he will await him in his palace; if a short stick falls he will know the worst. Then the lots were cast and the short stick fell to the ground. The Emperor "with a mingled cry of rage and despair, dashed the slip on the ground, exclaiming 'May this temple built by my ancestors evermore be accursed! Henceforward may every suppliant be denied what he entreats as I have been! Those that came in sorrow, may their sorrow be doubled; in happiness, may that happiness be changed to misery; in hope, may they meet despair; in health, sickness; in the pride of life and strength, death! I, Chung-ch'en, the last of the Mings, curse it.' "

So he went back to the palace and arranged for the death of himself and family. Next day, strangled with his own girdle, the last of the Mings lay dead on the Meishan in the Palace gardens at Peking.

When the news reached the commander-in-chief of the Chinese army, he gave the word which let in the Manchus into the heritage of the sons of Han.

CHAPTER II

THE REIGN OF SHUN CHIH

1644-1661.

The Manchu period—the Manchus—Nurha-chu—the Conquest—Wu San kwei—Accession of Shun chih—Ama Wang—Progress of the Conquest —Shang K'o hi—Chêng Che lung and Coxinga— Adam Schaal—Foreign relations—Death of Shun chih.

THE MANCHU PERIOD. Much more is popularly known of this period in Europe and America than of the dynasties which preceded it. This is natural both on account of its nearness to our own time and because of the necessarily closer relations established during this period with the western nations. Nevertheless, the history of the Manchu dynasty, like the history of China generally, has been written for the most part from the foreign standpoint and might perhaps be more justly entitled, as we have so far appreciated it a History of the foreign relations of China during the Manchu period. This result has followed from two obvious considerations. First, those who have written have been for the most part interested mainly in questions which concern the outer world. Secondly, the Chinese have followed the custom of deferring the publication of the memoirs of a dynasty until the dynasty itself has run its course. Hence on many points in the story of the epoch we have considerably less light from native sources than on the stories of the dynasties of Han or Sung. In our description of the events coming within this period we shall endeavor to preserve the same sense of proportion observed in the earlier volume. Many important questions must, of course, be treated less than adequately, but in these cases it will be easy to supply the deficiency from detailed and authoritative sources.

THE MANCHUS. The Kim Tatars, or Manchus, have already been described as a branch of the great Tatar family. They had their original home on the banks of the Sungari River. They make their first appearance upon the field of history in the 10th and 11th Centuries, when they followed the Khitan Tatars into the northern part of China. The Khitans had adopted the name of *Liao*, or *Iron*, as the title of their dynasty, and transmitted it to the peninsula which they wrested from the Chinese and which has ever since borne the name of *Liao-tung*. On their heels came the ancestors of the Manchus, then called *Nüchihs*, and, with a fling at their rivals, took the name *Kim*, or *gold*, for, said they, "Iron rusts, gold keeps its color." A century later, however, the Kim Tatars were driven out of China by Jenghiz

Khan. The name *Manchu*, or *Pure*, was given to the tribe by Aisin Gioro, who was miraculously born to a heavenly maiden in the Chang Pai mountains. Aisin Gioro consolidated the Manchu power and established his capital at Otoli, but after his reign, which was violently ended, the Manchus pass out of sight until the middle of the sixteenth century.

Nurhachu. We may perhaps usefully summarize what has already been said on the subject of the Manchu conquest and retrace the steps which led to the downfall of the Mings. The most potent instrument in the early stages of the conquest was the famous chief Nurhachu, who aspired to become a second Jenghiz Khan. Born in A. D. 1559, he succeeded in conquering the Liao-tung peninsula in A. D. 1582. From that moment onwards he cast covetous eyes upon the Ming dominions to the south. Contact with the Chinese seemed inevitably to create an atmosphere of conflict. The conflict became more and more embittered as the years passed, and Nurhachu, in issuing the famous declaration, known as the *"Seven Hates,"* showed that he was anxious to seek some justification for the projected campaign. At the same time, in taking the throne name of Tien Ming, he showed unmistakably that his intention was nothing less than conquest. This achievement was, in all probability, only averted by his death in A. D. 1627. The foresight which led him to send his son in early childhood into China that he might be instructed in the language, manners and customs of the Chinese, is only one more indication amongst many of the purpose which lay nearest to his heart.

THE CONQUEST. Hostile, however, as were the intentions of the Manchus, it is important to remember that, as on the earlier occasion under the Sungs, the actual occupation of China came to them as the result of an invitation from the Chinese themselves. Many years after, the Emperor Kang-hsi was able to say in his last Will and Testament: "Of all the dynasties which have succeeded up to the present, there is none which has acquired the Empire with so much right and justice as mine." The facts which give some color to this claim have already been recited. They may be briefly restated. On the death of Nurhachu the campaign against China was at once followed up by his son. The north was ravaged and Peking, where the Ming Emperor was living amid a horde of eunuchs and effeminate literati, was threatened. The expedition had already caused the "Son of Heaven" to lose face, and the people were ready to believe that the Mings were abandoned by Providence. But, as we have seen, the downfall came without the actual intervention of the Manchu. The rebellion of *Li Tsze-cheng* and his capture of Peking were the immediate causes of the suicide of the last of the Mings and the Empire lay apparently, at this juncture, at the mercy of the rebels.

Wu San-kwei. Now appears on the scene the great general who by some has been esteemed as the chief of patriots, while by others he has been regarded as the worst of traitors. In later years he was possibly not without his pangs of self-reproach, but it is only fair to give him credit throughout his career for the highest of motives. It was not tolerable to him to see the capital in the hands of rebels. There was at least a chance of securing peace for the Empire by calling in the Tatars. Wu San-kwei was near the frontier when, in A. D. 1643, he heard of the capture of Peking. He hurried to meet the victor, but, on attacking a certain stronghold, he was dismayed to find that Li held possession of his aged father, whom he threatened to slay under his son's eyes unless submission was made. No more touching story of loyalty has ever been written than that which tells how Wu San Kwei fell down on his knees and, bursting into tears, besought his father's pardon for sacrificing the tenderness of a son to loyalty towards his sovereign. The father was not behind the son in courage, and gave himself cheerfully to death while, as we have already told, vengeance was not long delayed. Of the subsequent history of Wu San kwei there will be something to say in the following chapters.

Accession of Shun Chih. The Tatar conqueror, Tsung têh, under these circumstances invited to occupy the vacant throne, lived just long enough to enter Peking. He died in A. D. 1644, after proclaiming as his successor the young prince who at the age of six assumed the title of *Shun chih* and is generally regarded as the first of the Manchu sovereigns of China. The dynastic title chosen was that of *Ta' Ts'ing*, or *Great Pure* Dynasty. According to the accounts given by the Jesuit fathers, China at this time contained a population of eleven and a half million families. At the end of the reign another estimate was made of nearly fifteen million families, or eighty-nine million individuals. The whole Empire was well mapped out by the Jesuits and Father Martini published in A. D. 1654 his *Atlas Sinensis*. Descriptions of the time show a remarkable degree of organization for the accommodation of officials on the public roads. An itinerary was printed, lodging places everywhere provided and runners went a day ahead to make all necessary preparations. The reign of Shun-chih is marked by the re-division of the land into eighteen provinces, instead of the fifteen which had existed under the Mings.

AMA WANG. For the greater part of the successful achievements of the early part of the reign of Shun chih the credit should be given to the Emperor's uncle, the Regent Ama Wang. His was the comprehensive intelligence and the strong arm which grasped and suppressed most of the dangerous outbreaks of rebellion and when he died, whilst on a hunting expedition, in A. D. 1651 the conquest had been to a large extent secured.   Shun chih showed less than gratitude.   A royal funeral was, indeed, celebrated and posthumous honors awarded, but a few months afterwards the tongue of slander reached the ears of Shun chih and, under the impression that Ama Wang had before his death been seeking his own aggrandizement the Emperor degraded his memory, destroyed his tomb, and even mutilated the dead body.

PROGRESS OF THE CONQUEST. The security of the Ta Ts'ing Dynasty was far from complete with the conquest of the north. The situation was not unlike that in England after the death of Harold at the Battle of Hastings. New pretenders to the Ming succession were constantly put forward and leaders were found to head the obstinate rebellions which broke out in various provinces. There were, too, many Portuguese from Macao ready to serve as mercenaries. Some of these were enlisted and promised to provide artillery, but jealousy of the foreigners proved a stronger passion than even hatred of the Manchu. The chief resistance to the invader was naturally in the south. At Nanking a great rally was made around the person of the prince *Fu Wang*, but the Chinese were defeated and the claimant drowned in the waters of the Yang tze River. Fu Wang was manifestly unfit to afford a promising rallying point since he was more given to the pursuit of pleasure than to the hardships of a soldier's life. It is told of him that on one occasion he sighed, and explained the sigh with the remark, "I am sighing to think it is impossible now-a-days to find a first rate actor." The General Che K'o Fa made another rally at Yang chow, which he defended heroically for some time. But the tide of massacre flowed on irresistibly. The "*Journal of a Citizen of Yang chow*" has been translated and gives a most harrowing picture from the pen of an eye witness of the butchery which went on until, as the writer tells us, ten or even a hundred Chinamen, meeting a single Manchu soldier, prostrated themselves and bent their necks for the sword without daring to flee. "If there are any," says Wang, in concluding one of the most terrible narratives ever written, "who, born in a period of peace and enjoying a tranquil life, have not in themselves wisdom enough to govern themselves aright, let them find in this narrative of events a lesson and a warning." One Ming princeling was put forward in Fuh Kien, another in Tcho Kiang, others in other places. But it was all in vain. One was captured and sent to Peking to be strangled with the bow-string. Another was slain in battle. Remorselessly the conquerers continued their advance. The siege of Che Kiang produced one memorable act of heroism on the part of the conquered when Lo Wang, pretending for the occasion to be a would-be Emperor, saved the city by the sacrifice of himself. In Kwang-si two Christian Chinese generals made another obstinate resistance, but again in vain. Canton, after an investment of ten months was captured and a horrible massacre took place in which over a hundred thousand persons perished. The last claimant to the Ming throne, Yungli, was encountered in the extreme southwest and was finally delivered up to the conquerors by the Burmese in the year of Shun chih's death. He and his son Constantine were slain and his wife and mother, Anne and Helena, who were Christians, were kept in prison in Yunnan fu until their death.

In addition to these attempts to restore the deposed dynasty Shun chih had to contend with a trouble of another kind in the rebellion in the west under *Si Wang*. This uprising deserves to be mentioned if only as an illustration of the fearful waste of human life which insurrections in China have entailed. The massacre of thirty thousand literati was only one incident in the career of Si Wang. The massacre of the wives was on a larger scale still. Si Wang believed that his army would be invincible if only his soldiers were freed from domestic ties. So at his bidding four hundred thousand women were slain. The sacrifice was useless, for the leader was soon after slain by an arrow and the rebellion melted away.

SHANG K'o HI. It is to be noted that many of the most famous generals in this terrible campaign of subjugation were Chinese rather than Manchu. Of these we have already mentioned

Wu San kwei, who for his services was made "Prince Pacifier of the West" with the Viceroyalty of Yunnan and Sze chuen and a residence at Singanfu. Another, almost equally famous, was *Shang K'o hi*, who passed from the service of the Mings in A. D. 1635 and remained for the rest of his life one of the most trusted servants of the Manchus. He was appointed Prince Pacifier of the South" in A. D. 1646 and had charge of the Manchu armies in Kwang tung which he governed until A. D. 1674. He was the principal leader in the attack on Canton. In later years many efforts were made to induce him to join in the rebellion of Wu San kwei, but he stood firm in his allegiance. When he heard of the defection of his son he was overwhelmed with grief and committed suicide.

Chêng Che lung and Coxinga. Two of the most romantic figures in the story of the conquest are those of the great pirates, Chêng Che lung and his son, Chêng Ch'êng Kung, better known as Coxinga, a corruption by the Portuguese of the title *Kwo-sing-ye*, "Possessor of the National Surname." The father was a native of the province of Fuh Kien, but had lived for many years in a Japanese settlement in Formosa where the son was born of a Japanese mother. The elder Chêng was first of all only an ordinary freebooter, but gradually he developed into a serious opponent of the Manchu supremacy and the conquerors had more difficulty with him and his apparently omnipresent fleet than with all the land forces of China. The son earned an even more terrible name and became to the Manchu what Hereward the Wake was to the Norman. On one occasion four thousand Manchus were made prisoners after a naval battle and were liberated with their ears and noses cut off. They were ordered slain by the shamed and indignant Emperor. The terror of Coxinga at length became so great that the people of six provinces were ordered to retire three leagues inland under pain of death, after destroying all their property, in order to leave to the pirates nothing but a desert shore. The effect was felt as painfully by the peaceful inhabitants as by the pirates, for many thousands who had hitherto got their living by fishing were now ruined. One of the most important achievements of Coxinga was the driving out of the Dutch from Formosa, after a long siege of Fort Zealandia, and the assumption of sovereignty over the island. The new principality drew colonies from the province of Fuh Kien, and Formosa remained an appanage of the "Sea Quelling Duke" for some twenty-eight years. After many adventures the father fell into the hands of the Manchus and was executed in Peking in A. D. 1661. The son survived only one year, dying at the age of thirty-nine after a most romantic career. His adventures form the subject of one of the best known of Japanese plays by the dramatist Chikamatsu. It is interesting to add that the descendents of Coxinga were ennobled under the title of *Hai-ching-king* (Sea Quelling Duke) presumably for their services in restoring the island of Formosa to the Empire.

ADAM SCHAAL. The entry of the Jesuits into China under the Mings has already been recorded. Matteo Ricci had come as early as A. D. 1601 and had lived without undue friction with the Chinese until his death in A. D. 1610. His place was filled by Longobardi, and others came whose scientific zeal produced over three hundred treatises on various branches of western learning. The most commanding figure among the members of the order was a German, the famous Adam Schaal, who, arriving in A. D. 1628, survived the dynasty and lived on into the reign of Kang hsi. He was chosen by the Manchus to reform the Calendar and in addition to his scientific work made many converts. During the minority of Kang hsi he incurred the jealousy of the regents and was cast into prison, dying of grief and suffering on Aug. 16, 1669, after thirty-seven years of splendid work in the Imperial service. During the reign of Shunchih he stood in high favor at court, although even then the quarrels between Dominicans and Jesuits and the events taking place in Japan were making the position of the missionaries precarious.[1]

FOREIGN RELATIONS. The arrival of Europeans had, even before the end of the Ming Dynasty, begun to exercise a disturbing influence on the course of Chinese history. The relations of the *Dutch* had commenced with the attack on Macao and the occupation of the Pescadores in A. D. 1622. The Chinese had met the situation with the shrewd suggestion that Holland should take Formosa rather than the Pescadores and the hint had been accepted. Formosa remained Dutch till Coxinga expelled the intruders and made the island his own. Several embassies were attempted by the pushing Hollanders of this time. In A. D. 1653 they sent an Embassy to Canton which was brought to naught by the alertness of their Portuguese rivals. Two years later, an Embassy was sent to Peking and an interesting account has come down to us from the pen of Niewhof, who has detailed for us some of the astonishing servilities which were exacted of the accommodating ambassadors. By their complacency, however, they secured the privilege of sending an Embassy once in eight years and of employing four ships in the Chinese trade. There were to be only a hundred men in a Company and only twenty were to be permitted to proceed to Court.

Russian efforts were even more persistent. As early as A. D. 1567 two Cossacks had attempted to see the Emperor but had failed because they brought no presents. In A. D. 1619 Evashto Pettlin arrived at Peking with the same intention, but he too brought no presents and was dismissed without seeing the dragon's face. He got, however, a letter which no one in Moscow was able to decipher. In A. D. 1640 the Russian conquests on the Amur brought them into close relations with the Middle Kingdom and in A. D. 1653 the Czar Alexis sent Baikoff who was too proud to *kotow* before Shun chih and was thereupon dismissed. Persistent expeditions followed, extending into the next reign, viz.: in A. D. 1658, 1672 and 1677. The ultimate result was the Treaty of Nertchinsk in A. D. 1689—the first treaty ever agreed upon by the court at Peking in modern times.

English influence was of little account during the reign of Shunchih. The visit of Capt. Weddell in A. D. 1635 has already been alluded to. The arrival of another power was naturally viewed by the Portuguese with something more than coldness and there was little encouragement for British enterprise from any other quarter until after the close of the reign.

Among foreign affairs we may with some reason reckon the visit of the *Grand Lama* of Tibet, since Tibet had not yet become a part of the Chinese Empire. On the arrival of this august personage at Peking Shunchih conferred upon him the title of Dalai Lama which has since been borne by the ecclesiastical heads of Lamaism. The term had indeed been used by the Mongol Khans for the Tibetan ruler as early as A. D. 1576, but the confirmation of that title by Shunchih in 1653 made its authority complete.

DEATH OF SHUN CHIH. The first Manchu Emperor of China made serious efforts to secure popularity among his new subjects. He showed himself as much as possible among the people and ratified as far as possible the existing Chinese laws. He retained the Six Boards, accepted the counsels of the literati, and, in the interests of the old order, refused permission to the Chinese to learn the Tatar language. On the other hand, the insistence on the wearing of the *queue* as a badge of subjection to the Manchu provoked the intensest resentment. The Chinese were as inordinately attached to their national manner of wearing the hair long and unshaven as the Koreans were of their top-knot at the time of the Japanese occupation of the peninsula. Hence when the order came to shave the head with the exception of one long lock at the back there were thousands of people who preferred to lose their lives rather than dishonor their heads. In some provinces, such as Fuh kien, the resistance lasted until recent times and the general willingness to sacrifice the pigtails exhibited in the recent revolution has shown that even centuries are not sufficient to recommend a fashion against the sentiment of a nation.

Shun chih's death took place in A. D. 1661, according to one account from small-pox, but, according to another and more circumstantial one, from grief at the decease of a favorite wife. This wife had been the spouse of a young Manchu whom the Emperor summoned to Court and, with malice prepense, boxed his ears. Of course the insulted subject could not with honor survive the indignity and, on his suicide, which had been foreseen, Shun chih at once married the widow. When she died the grief-stricken Emperor was with difficulty prevented from slaying himself. He had thirty women immolated, according to the old fashion, at her tomb and preserved the body, reduced to ashes, in a silver urn. Then he shaved his head and went, like a madman, from pagoda to pagoda till death ensued. Just before his death he selected as his heir his second son, then eight years old,—destined to bear the great and glorious name of Kang hsi. He then exclaimed, "I shall soon depart to rejoin my ancestors," and expired at the age of twenty-four after a reign of eighteen years. The four appointed regents at once repaired to the ancestral hall and vowed before the shades of the dead to be loyal to the trust imposed upon them. So commenced the reign of Kang hsi.

NOTES

1.   The life of Adam Schaal is given by Rémusat in his *"Melanges Asiatiques"* Vol II, p. 217.

CHAPTER III

THE REIGN OF KANG HSI

A. D. 1661—1722

Accession—Rebellion of Wu San kwei—The Jesuit Missions—The Advance of Russia—War with the Eleuths—The Sacred Edict—P'u Sung ling —The Reforms of Kang hsi—Death of Kang hsi.

ACCESSION. Shunchih was succeeded by his second son who took the name of Kang hsi, a title signifying *Unalterable Peace,* and inaugurated, if not a period of peace, at any rate one of the longest and most splendid eras in the history of China. The reign completed a full Chinese cycle of sixty years and was for fifty-four years contemporary with that of Louis XIV—a fact of which the French Jesuits have not been slow to remind us. It was also for nearly half a century coincident with the reign of the great Mogul of India, Aurungzib. For the first six years of this long period Kang hsi was under the control of four somewhat reactionary regents, but, on the death of one of them, the Emperor, who was now fourteen years old, determined to assume for himself

27

the reins of government. He began with characteristic vigor to purge the court of the unwholesome influence of the palace eunuchs. Four thousand of these pestilent parasites were expelled and their employment strictly prohibited for the future,—a prohibition, alas, but slackly observed. The Emperor then ordered the laws of the Empire to be newly engraved on iron tablets of a thousand pounds' weight and prepared to rule as well as to reign. Kang hsi is described in the following terms: "Fairly tall and well proportioned, he loved all manly exercises and devoted three months annually to hunting. Large bright eyes lighted up his face, which was pitted with small pox. Contemporary observers vie in praising his wit, understanding, and liberality of mind. Indefatigable in government, he kept a careful watch on his Ministers, his love for the people leading him to prefer economy to taxation. He was personally frugal, yet on public works he would lavish large sums." [1]

THE REBELLION OF WU SAN KWEI. The final steps in the pacification of China belong to this reign, such as the suppression of the piratical raids of Coxinga, but at one time it seemed very much as though the whole work of conquest would have to be done over again through the defection of the great Chinese general, Wu San Kwei. "The Pacificator of the West" had for a long time been regarded almost as an independent feudatory chief, and may very well in this respect have incurred the suspicion of the Emperor. When an invitation, offered as a test, came from Kang hsi to pay a visit to Peking, Wu Sang Kwei had on his part excuse for suspicion, especially as his son, who was then residing in the capital, advised him against compliance. The only alternative to obedience, however, was rebellion. "I will go to Peking," he declared, "if they persist, but it will be at the head of eighty thousand men." So the breach came and each side at once took the inevitable step of making war. The partisans of Wu San Kwei formed a plot in Peking to blow up all the Manchu court at the New Year festival. This was discovered on the very eve of the day appointed through the treason of a slave. All hope of reconciliation was now at an end. The outlook for the Manchus seemed at first black, for four provinces at once declared for Wu San Kwei and the whole of the Southwest was seething with disaffection. There was, moreover, a strong disposition on the part of the Mongols of Tartary, under a leader who was reputed to be descended from Jenghiz Khan, to make common cause with the Chinese. To add to Kang hsi's troubles a great earthquake and fire desolated Peking and destroyed the Imperial Palace. Nevertheless the young Emperor faced the all but desperate situation with \characteristic coolness and courage. The Manchu garrisons held their own and gradually Wu San Kwei was forced into a position where defeat became more or less inevitable. The struggle lasted for four years, during which time the Manchus were greatly assisted by the new artillery which had been manufactured under the instruction of the Jesuit missionaries. Death came to the heroic rebel in A. D. 1678 or 1679 just when he was at the end of his resources. Then he who had never known defeat for fifty years of strenuous warfare yielded to a stronger foe than Kang hsi. It was deemed right by the victor to make an example of the vanquished even though the grave had claimed him. Wu San Kwei's bones were divided and sent into all the provinces in order that they might be hung from a gallows and treated with contumely by the populace.[2] Opinions will always vary as to whether Wu San Kwei should be honored or execrated by his fellow countrymen. A charitable judgment will scarcely hesitate to think of him as having throughout acted according to his conscience and as deserving the name of a brave and patriotic Chinaman.

The Jesuit Missions. The guardians of the young king were from the first ill-disposed towards the missionaries, and this for more than religious reasons. They regarded with extreme jealousy the disposition of the Emperor to trust (not without cause) the superior ability of the foreigners in the matter of calendar-making and astronomical science. Adam Schaal was thrown into prison and condemned to death by slicing (*ling-chih*), but fortunately the sentence was cancelled before it was too late. However, the venerable priest never came forth from his dungeon and died Aug. 16, 1669, at the age of seventy-eight, having given thirty-seven years of distinguished service to the Emperors of China. Others suffered a similar fate, the Dutch Jesuit Verbiest, escaping from confinement only when Kang hsi took up the reins. The Emperor, it is said, was annoyed at the errors of the court astronomers and only too glad to fill the vacancy caused by the death of Adam Schaal by the appointment of Verbiest. Louis XIV recognized the honor which Kang hsi had conferred upon the Jesuit scientist by the gift of a large bronze azimuth and celestial globe for the Emperor's use. These remained prominent objects upon the city walls of the capital till Peking was looted by the Allied troops in 1900. The astronomical instruments were taken by the Germans and afterwards displayed among the treasures of Potsdam. At the same time Kang hsi was by no means indifferent to the religious side of the situation and might have been sympathetically affected had it not been for the unfortunate differences between the missionaries themselves. In China, as in Japan, the work of the Jesuits had been followed up by other orders, such as the Franciscans and Dominicans, and these had differed more than a little in matters of policy if not in matters of doctrine. These differences were accentuated by the arrival of Bishop Maigrot, whose ignorance of Chinese excited the contempt of Kang hsi, and whose opposition to the work of the earlier missionaries was open and illiberal. The appointment of a Papal Legate added fuel to the fire and Kanghsi found himself under the necessity of banishing De Tournon, the aforesaid legate, to Macao. The question of ancestor worship was one chief cause of controversy, the Jesuits regarding it as not wholly irreconcilable with Christianity, the Dominicans insisting on its absolute discontinuance. Another question was that of the term to be used as an equivalent for "God," and incredible bitterness was aroused by what one would have supposed a matter to be critically and dispassionately considered.[3] We have an echo of this situation in the words of the good Pope in Browning's *"Ring and the Book"*:—

"Five years since in the Province of To kien,
 Which is in China as some people know,
 Maigrot, my Vicar-Apostolic there,
 Having a great qualm, issues a decree.
 Alack, the converts use as God's name, not
 Tien-chu but plain *Tien* or else mere *Shang-ti*,
 As Jesuits please to fancy politic,
 While say Dominicans, it calls down fire,—
 For *Tien* means Heaven, and *Shang-ti,* supreme
     prince,
 While *Tien-chu* means the lord of heaven."

Kang hsi was scandalized, not only by the quarrels which these controversies provoked among professors of the same faith, but perhaps even more by the fact that the Pope decided for one party, the Dominicans, while *he* had already decided for the Jesuits. Such an interference with his supremacy, ecclesiastical and civil, boded ill, he thought, for the Empire, and from this time onward his attitude was more or less hostile. It should, however, be said that there was no lack of deliberateness in the matter and many meetings of the Council were held to give opportunity for discussion. The emphasis, moreover, in the proscriptive edicts which followed was invariably on the political character of the missionaries' work, rather than on its religious aspect. "False and pernicious doctrine" they regarded it indeed, but it was with the fear of foreign political interference in their hearts that they formed their estimate. The Emperor himself was certainly not ungrateful for the labors of the Jesuits, especially those of a scientific character. Verbiest's work, *"The Perpetual Astronomy of the Emperor Kang hsi,"* enjoyed a high reputation. The Jesuits, Bouvet, Régis, Jarboux, Fridelli, Cardoso, de Tartré, de Mailla and Bonjour, rendered inestimable service through their cartography of the provinces. The maps were printed in the great work of du Halde and were not only useful to the Empire but formed the first introduction to modern Europe of some knowledge of things Chinese. It may be asserted without fear of contradiction that the advanced position attained by France in Sinology to-day is largely due to the interest created in China by the work of the early Jesuit fathers. In this respect Colbert's statesmanship and the foresight of the French Academy of Sciences have been amply rewarded.

In A. D. 1692, after twenty-two years of proscription, prejudice was so far allayed that a declaration, to which the Emperor gave the force of law, was published, reciting the advantages which missionary enterprise had brought to China and giving permission to the missionaries to remain. This tolerant attitude was maintained until A. D. 1717 when a certain mandarin whose travels had made him only too well acquainted with the situation in Japan and the Philippines, solemnly warned the Emperor of the vaulting ambition of the foreign propagandists. This led to the renewal of the prohibition against preaching as the sole means available for warding off mischievous complications.

THE ADVANCE OF RUSSIA. Kang hsi's management of affairs in the south has already been described. By A. D. 1684 even Formosa, a perennial source of trouble, had been won from the grandson of the great pirate. In the meantime trouble was brewing beyond the northern and western frontiers. For some time the advance of Russia eastward had exercised a disquieting influence upon the tribes of Central Asia. From A. D. 1582 when the robber Cossack, Yermak, set out from Perm in charge of an expedition organized

by the Strogonoffs, there had been stealthy but
ceaseless progress in the Russianization of Northern Asia.   The Yenizei was reached in A. D. 1620.
In 1630 Tobolsk was settled.   In 1648, after a
successful war with the Tunguses and Buriats,
Russian dominion was extended to Lake Baikal.
With headquarters on the Lena, four thousand
miles from Moscow, trade and conquest still pushed
on.   The great explorer, Poyarkoff, discovered a
tributary of the Amur in A. D. 1643.   He encountered little opposition from the Manchus, who
at this time were too busy with their invasion of
China, so he entered the Sungari and at last came
upon the Amur, to the mouth of which he drifted.
Poyarkoff appealed in vain to his government for
men to follow up his discoveries, but private enterprise responded in the person of Khabaroff.
The new colonists alienated many of the natives
by their overbearing manner, and in A. D. 1658
experienced a severe defeat at the hands of the
Chinese, who carried back a number of captives
to Peking.   It is said that the descendants of the
captives are still to be distinguished by their un-
Chinese features, and that they live in the very
section of Peking to which they were originally
consigned.   In A. D. 1689 came the signing of
the *Treaty of Nerchinsk*, already alluded to.
This famous agreement secured peace between the
two nations for a period of one hundred and sixty
years.   There was no further extension of Russian influence in China during the reign of

Kang hsi.   Peter the Great sent an embassy under Ismailoff in A. D. 1719 which was graciously received, but a second expedition failed because it found Kang hsi on his death-bed and the anti-foreign ministers in control.   Thus ended Peter's dream of "tapping the wealth of China."

WAR WITH THE ELEUTHS.   Among the tribes made restless by the Russian advances were the Eleuths, a tribe of Kalmucks whose leader, Galdan, seems to have dreamed, like others before and since, of repeating the career of Jenghiz Khan. He took it for granted that an alliance with Russia must furnish a good opportunity for breaking with China and would compel that country to recognize his independence.   The Emperor drew the sword reluctantly, and after trying various means of conciliation; but he was determined to bring Galdan to his senses.   The war ended in A. D. 1690 with the pretended submission of Galdan and, the following year, the Emperor, accompanied by the Jesuit Gerbillon, who was a good Mongolian and Russian scholar, held a review of the troops in the field.   Unfortunately, Galdan's ambitions revived and a new campaign was rendered necessary in A. D. 1697.   An ultimatum was despatched to the too audacious chieftain and a limit of seventy days assigned, but before the expiration of this period Galdan was released from his predicament by death.   He is said to have poisoned himself.   It must be added that the Eleuth chief showed in the conduct of his cam-

paigns very little resemblance to the great conqueror whom he desired to emulate. A nephew,
Tsi Wang, tried for a while to deserve better success, but a third Chinese force penetrated Mongolia and Kang hsi had the good fortune to cele-
brate the complete, subjugation of the Eleuths
on the sixtieth anniversary of his ascending the
Dragon throne.

No other trouble beyond the frontier vexed the
reign of Kang hsi, with the exception of the dispute in Tibet between the two factions of Lamas,
known as the Red Caps and the Yellow Caps. A
garrison was sent to watch events and Chinese
authority was, as we shall see, ultimately recognized.

KANG HSI AND LITERATURE. Notwithstanding
the demands made upon him by long-contin-
ued rebellion and warfare, Kang hsi may be regarded as one of the most munificent patrons Chinese literature ever possessed. Through his efforts and encouragement some stupendous literary
enterprises were brought to a successful consum-
mation. Of these the works most deserving of
mention are two large concordances printed in
forty-four and thirty-six volumes respectively; an
encyclopædia in forty-four volumes; another, il-
lustrated, in sixteen hundred and twenty-eight
volumes of two hundred pages each; and, chief in
fame if not in importance, the great Dictionary
containing 44,439 characters arranged under the
two hundred and fourteen radicals. This was the

work of thirty literati who were kept busy for a number of years. For the printing of Government publications Kang hsi ordered the engraving of 250,000 copper types.

THE SACRED EDICT. The *Shun Yu*, or Sacred Edict, is perhaps the best known of the writings attributed personally to Kang hsi. It consists of sixteen maxims, corresponding with the sixteen years of the youthful sovereign who composed them. Each maxim consists of seven ideographs and the whole is proclaimed twice a month. It is supposed to be committed to memory and a versified form has been issued for the use of children. These sixteen moral maxims, which, as Dr. Giles observes, are commonplace enough in themselves, are as follows:

1. Pay attention to filial and fraternal duties.
2. Pay respect to kindred, and display the excellence of harmony.
3. Prevent litigation in your neighborhood.
4. Pay attention to husbandry and the culture of the mulberry.
5. Exercise economy in the use of money.
6. Magnify scholarship and academical learning.
7. Oppose foreign religions in the interest of orthodoxy.
8. Explain the laws.
9. Manifest politeness of manners.
10. Attend to the essential employments.
11. Attend to the instruction of youth.

12. Secure the innocent from false accusation.
13. Warn those who hide deserters.
14. Pay taxes without frequent urging.
15. Extirpate robbery and theft.
16. Settle animosities in the interest of life.

The issuing of the *Shun Yu* may perhaps be best regarded as the effort of an enthusiastic boy, placed in a position of great responsibility, and anxious to do something towards promoting a return to the virtues of the "good old times."

P'U SUNG LING. With the encouragement of the Emperor it may readily be supposed that many would be disposed to try their own hand at literature. This is indeed the case, although the most famous works of the reign belong to a category not highly regarded by the literati, viz.: the Novel. The *"Strange Stories"* of *P'u Sung ling*, to take only one example, are exceedingly entertaining. The writer was born in A. D. 1622, took his first degree in 1641 and completed the book by which he is known in 1679. For some years it circulated only in manuscript, as the author was too poor to have it printed. The printed work did not appear till 1740. As illustrating the variety of interest in the *"Strange Stories,"* we may quote Dr. Giles.[4] "There is a Rip Van Winkle story, with the pathetic return of the hero to find, as the Chinese poet says—

"City and suburb as of old,
But hearts that loved us long since cold."

There is a sea-serpent story and a story of a big bird or rukh; also a story about a Jonah, who, in obedience to an order flashed by lightning on the sky when the junk was about to be swamped in a storm, was transferred by his fellow-passengers to a small boat, and cut adrift. So soon as the unfortunate victim had collected his senses and could look about him, he found that the junk had capsized and that every soul had been drowned."

THE REFORMS OF KANG HSI. The Emperor during his reign made many earnest attempts at reform. Among these was the effort to suppress the practice of *foot-binding* among the women. The origin of the practice, which is unknown to the Manchu women and to the Hakkas of the south, is doubtful. Some ascribe it to the desire to remove reproach from a certain club-footed Empress. Some see its origin in feminine envy of the "lily" feet of a famous royal mistress; and others again in the masculine desire to prevent the ladies of the household from gadding about. It is possible also that the practice was meant to show immunity from (and therefore superiority to) the necessity of field labor, as in the case of the long fingernails of the men. In any case it has been the cause of untold sufferings and Kang hsi's effort was one in the direction of real humanity. Custom, however, was too strong for the royal command or the example of the Manchu women to overcome. It is said that even to-day, after all the efforts of the "Anti-foot-binding Societies" there are still seventy million women in China with bound feet.

More successful was Kang hsi in the prohibition of the *immolation of women* at the funerals of the great.   Shun chih, it will be remembered, had sacrificed thirty slave-women at the tomb of his favorite.   Under similar circumstances, Kang hsi intervened to prevent the destruction of four, and his wishes were in this respect complied with.

The abolition of the *Capitation* tax was a very popular reform and did not a little towards allaying Chinese disaffection in many of the provinces. The people were also gratified by the return of the lands of which they had been unjustly deprived and even criminals, banished to the north, had reason to bless the Emperor who decided that, on account of the misery inflicted by the great heat upon travelers in the months from July to November, the transportations should cease during this period.

We may add to this account of the reforms of Kang hsi that the Emperor justly prided himself upon the "*royal rice,*" a species which he discovered could be cultivated as far north as Peking, and which he therefore believed must add to the welfare of his subjects.

DEATH OF KANG HSI.   In A. D. 1722 the aged sovereign celebrated an unique festival in the Palace of the Heavenly Purity.   It was the sixtieth year of his reign, and therefore marked the completion of a cycle of rule.   In honor of the occasion Kang hsi invited all men in the Empire over sixty years of age to be his guests at Peking. How many found it possible to accept we know not, but the occasion cannot have lacked interest and picturesqueness. Soon after the conclusion of the festivities Kang hsi went beyond the Great Wall to hunt leopards. While on this expedition he took cold and died, after a brief illness, on Dec. 20, 1722.

Thus ended what was without question a great reign. It amply justified the confidence with which Shun chih had regarded him when as a child he marked him out for sovereignty It may well also excuse the note of satisfaction expressed in Kang hsi's last Will and Testament:

"I, the Emperor, have more than a hundred sons and grandsons and I am aged seventy years. Kings, nobles, officers, soldiers, peoples, even the Mongols and others besides, bear witness to the attachment they bear for my person, regretting to see me so advanced in years. Under circumstances so flattering, if I am about to finish my long career, I shall leave life with satisfaction."

Notwithstanding, however, this satisfaction with the past, Kang hsi was not without forebodings in respect to the future, and the sagacity and foresight of a great ruler were never better manifested, than in the words he uttered in 1717:

"There is cause for apprehension, lest in the centuries or millenniums to come, China may be endangered by collisions with the various nations of the West who come hither from beyond the seas."

For this danger China had not to wait millenniums, and subsequent chapters will make plain the accuracy of the great Emperor's anticipation.

NOTES

1. Giles "Chinese Literature," p. 385.

2. Wu San kwei is still "officially venerated in Yunnan and we may see on each side of the bronze pagoda a gigantic sword, which was supposed to represent his arms, accompanied by laudatory inscriptions. There are many legends relating to Wu San Kwei; one, which is generally believed, is to the effect that his body has never been buried, but reposes in a silver coffin hanging from the ceiling of a secret chamber in the palace of the Viceroy; and on the day on which it touches the ground the Manchu dynasty will fall." Vicomte d'Ollone, *"In Forbidden China,"* p. 161. This legend conflicts with the account of the desecration of his bones.

3. In a prefatory note to a printed report of Dr. Legge's essay on "Confucianism in relation to Christianity" read at a Missionary Conference in 1877 I find the following words: "It was read in full assembly, but the Conference by a vote decided to omit it from the printed record of proceedings, in deference to the wishes of those who regarded it as taking one side in the controversy respecting the term to be used for God in the Chinese language."

4. Giles, "Chinese Literature," p. 352.

CHAPTER IV

THE REIGN OF YUNG CHENG

A. D. 1722-1736.

*Accession of Yung chêng—Secret Societies—
Insurrections—Foreign affairs—Edict against the
Missionaries—the Reforms of Yung chêng—
Yung chêng as author—the Great Earthquake—
Death.*

ACCESSION OF YUNG CHÊNG. Kang hsi had not
been altogether without his anxieties as to the succession. The eldest son was suspected of using
unholy arts to prevent the throne from descending to any but himself. The second son, the favorite of his father, was regarded as the victim
of these arts and was, in consequence, out of his
mind. It was not till the last day of his life that
the Emperor could bring himself to nominate an
heir. This was Yung chêng, a man of good ability and mature years, being forty-four at the time
of his father's death. The story has been circulated that the new monarch was really the four-
teenth and not the fourth son and that the fourth,
then in Mongolia, was arrested and imprisoned,
but the report is probably without foundation.

Yung chêng in any case took pains at the outset to make good his title to the throne-name he had chosen—*Stable Peace*.

SECRET SOCIETIES. The most serious difficulties to be encountered by Yung chêng, difficulties which unfortunately increased during the succeeding reigns, sprang out of the multiplication and spread of Secret Societies. Anti-dynastic movements had ceased to make open insurrection, but, in concealing themselves from the notice of the authorities, they became "hidden fires," and the anti-Manchu spirit succeeded in organizing itself in manifold ways. The capacity of the Chinese for organization along these lines has been frequently noted, yet possibly no one has really succeeded in getting to the bottom of a very special and complex subject.[1] The best known of these associations into which the *"esprits forts"* of anti-Manchuism gathered themselves are those named the *White Lotus*, the *Triads* and the *Heaven and Earth* society.

The *White Lotus* society is said by some to go back to the fourth century, but seems really to have been organized in the first years of the Mongol dynasty. The founder of the Ming dynasty is said to have been affiliated. It reached the height of its influence at the end of the 18th Century. The *Triads* were possibly founded in Mongol times by the so-called "boxing monks" of Chao lin sz. The *Heaven and Earth* society was perhaps founded by the pirate Coxinga.

It is worth noting that there was an extensive employment of literature to further the aims of these secret orders. Especially was this the case with novels. *"The Dream of the Red Chamber"* [2] is a work of this character, one of the most widely read novels in all Chinese literature.

INSURRECTIONS. Antagonism to the dynasty, or at least to Yung chêng, showed itself not only in the sapping and undermining work of secret societies, but also in the open insurrections in more than one quarter. One of the earliest of these was that under a chief named Lo-puh, in Tsing hai. Over two hundred thousand men, largely Buddhist monks, were induced to throw in their lot with the movement, but General Nien so vigorously pushed the campaign against the rebels that it was in the course of a short time completely crushed. The rebel leader was once surprised in bed and only succeeded in escaping by disguising himself in a woman's clothes. The crushing of the rebellion was followed up by an imperial edict to the effect that from henceforth no monastery should contain more than three hundred monks and that these should not be permitted to carry arms.

A second and more serious rebellion broke out in A. D. 1726 in the southwest provinces of Kwei-chau, Sze ch'uen and Yunnan. It was brought about mainly by the independent attitude of the aboriginal tribes, and the chief purpose of the three years' campaign of subjugation was to establish more completely the Imperial rule over these semi-barbarous clans. This was accomplished through the skill and valor of the Chinese generals and soldiers, though not without the expenditure of much treasure and human life.

The war with the Eleuths, over whom Galdan Chering was now ruling in the room of his father, was not prosecuted during this reign, and the Chinese forces were withdrawn from the desert of Gobi.

Foreign Affairs. With the outside nations the relations of China continued much as in the preceding reign. With *Portugal* matters made little or no advance. Père Magaillans, who had in the previous reign been "loaden for four whole months together with nine chains, three about his neck, his arms and his legs," but who had, like the Apostle Paul, been delivered by a great earthquake, an earthquake which shook all Peking, returned to China about A. D. 1723 with a letter from the Pope, and was permitted to have an audience with the Emperor. The only result was the humiliation of the envoys who were represented as belonging to "the subject nations." Moreover, the citizens of Macao were not too well pleased with the necessity of paying for the thirty chests of presents which had been graciously accepted by the Emperor.

The *Russian* Embassy, which was sent by the Empress Catherine in A. D. 1727, was more fortunate. A mission consisting of six ecclesiastics and four laymen was permitted to remain at Peking for the purpose of studying the Chinese and Manchu languages. It was arranged that the *personnel* of the mission should be changed every ten years and the Emperor seems to have jumped at the chance of getting interpreters from elsewhere than the Order of Jesus. The caravan trade was also regulated, and the treaty signed August A. D. 1727, which continued in force till June, 1858, is said by Dr. Williams to be the longest-lived treaty on record.

EDICT AGAINST THE MISSIONARIES. The literati began from the commencement of the reign of Yung chêng to push their opposition to the "Religion of the Lord of Heaven," and presented a memorial soon after his accession petitioning for the banishment of the foreign priests and the conversion of the churches to "other and better uses." Perhaps the Emperor himself was inclined to anti-foreign opinions, and the fact that certain members of the royal family, who seemed possible rivals to himself, had embraced Christianity, made his inclination the more pronounced. But indeed he seemed to be genuinely concerned lest China should become Christian. He was a votary of a foreign religion himself, being a daily worshiper of the Buddha, but he contemplated with something like consternation the prospect of a Christian China. "You wish," he said, "that all the Chinese should become Christians, and indeed your creed commands it. I am well aware of this, but in that event what would become of us? Should we not soon be merely the subjects of your kings?" Consequently, a hostile edict was issued in 1724 and the missionaries obeyed the decree of banishment to the extent of retiring to Canton, leaving three hundred thousand converts well-nigh shepherdless. Some attempt on the part of a few of the priests to return to their flocks was met with sterner measures, and in 1732 all the priests who could be "rounded up" were deported to the Portuguese possession of Macao.

THE REFORMS OF YUNG CHÊNG. In spite of the severe measures adopted against the propagation of Christianity, the missionaries themselves are loud in their testimony to the general justice and beneficence of Yung chêng's reign. He was, they said, indefatigable in work, and was ever ready to recognize merit and reward virtue. Among the reforms he introduced was one to limit to the Emperor himself the right to sign a *sentence of death*. Like Tai tsung of the T'ang dynasty, he desired the greatest possible deliberation in a matter of such importance and required that the case should be presented to him three times, lest in the first instance he should be tempted to act impulsively.

To encourage *agriculture* he made a law that in future the taxes should be paid by the proprietors, instead of by the tenants of the land. Still more significant was the remarkable order given in 1732 that in future the city governor should annually supply him with the name of the peasant who had been most diligent in cultivating the soil, in preserving the unity of the family and in frugality and temperance of life. Such model peasants were to be made mandarins of the eighth class, with a right to wear the mandarin's robe, to sit in the presence of the Governor and to take tea with him. On their death, moreover, they were to be awarded the crowning glory of having their names inscribed in the Halls of the Ancestors.

YUNG CHÊNG AS AUTHOR. Possibly on the principle that "what one does through another one does himself," Yung chêng is to be numbered among the authors of China. To begin with, he has the credit, filial perhaps rather than literary, of amplifying and commenting on the *Sacred Edicts* of Kang hsi. In the next place, he is held responsible for a truly remarkable *Treatise on War*. It is entitled the *"Ten Precepts"* and was designed to secure in perpetuity the prestige and permanence of Manchu sovereignty. These precepts may be briefly summarized as follows:

1. Fathers and mothers to have tender care of their children.
2. Children to be subordinate to parents and the younger children to the elder.
3. Good relations to be maintained with all the world.
4. Parents to instruct children to obey the laws and to have respect for magistrates.

5. Soldiers to occupy themselves with the cultivation of the land.
6. Soldiers to render themselves skilful with bow and arrows, on foot and on horseback.
7. Soldiers to be economical, especially in the matter of marriages and funerals.
8. Soldiers to avoid excesses in wine.
9. Soldiers to avoid gambling.
10. Soldiers to be careful of life, by avoiding fights, homicides, duels and the like.

Truly, we have here a "military treatise" which, if followed to the letter, would go a long way towards rendering war impossible.

THE GREAT EARTHQUAKE. Earthquakes are recorded in previous reigns as working havoc in and around Peking. A very serious one visited the capital in the reign of Kang hsi. But the earthquake which visited Peking in 1730 all but destroyed the city. It is said that in a few minutes a hundred thousand persons were buried in the ruins. The Imperial Palace fared no better than the huts of the common people. There was general misery, in the midst of which the Emperor came nobly to the front. He gave liberally of his own private means, already strained by the terrible floods which had devastated the land prior to the earthquake, for the relief of the sufferers, and, strange as the fact may appear in the light of the Edict of 1724, a thousand ounces of gold were bestowed upon the Christian missionaries who remained in the northern capital to enable them to repair the damage done to the churches. It is a pleasant reflection that in calamity most people are able to put aside their prejudices and to learn a larger outlook upon humanity.

DEATH OF YUNG CHÊNG. Yung chêng died Oct. 5, 1735, after a "highly creditable" reign. He had just given audience to his ministers when he was taken ill. He died so suddenly that he had no opportunity to nominate his successor.

NOTES

1. See for "Secret Societies," Stanton, Pickering, Groot ("Sectarianism and Persecution in China") and an article by A. Maybon, *"Mercure de France,"* June 1912.

2. Giles, "Chinese Literature," pp. 350 ff.

CHAPTER V

THE REIGN OF KIEN LUNG

A. D. 1736-1796.

Kien lung—Attitude towards Christianity—Rebellion in Southwest—War in Central Asia—The Flight of a Tatar Tribe—War in Burmah—Conquest of the Miao-tsz—War in Tibet—Formosa—The Macartney Mission—The Dutch Mission—Kien lung and Literature—Festivities—The Abdication of Kien lung.

KIEN LUNG. Hung li, the fourth son of Yung chêng, ascended the throne under the title of *Kien lung*. The royal name, bestowed, according to the Chinese custom, after death, was Kao tsung. Although twenty-five years old, he at once appointed four regents upon whose counsel he might rely. At first this was taken to imply that he was disinclined to the cares and responsibilities of rulership, and desirous rather of devoting his days to the studies to which his father's wishes, as well as his own leanings, disposed him. But the marvelous energy which he displayed just as soon as he did assume the reins of government quickly dissipated these apprehensions and, although his early devotion to study continued throughout life, it was but as one of many means for equipping himself for the tremendous task laid upon him. His accession was marked by a striking act of clemency, rare enough in Oriental annals. The princes of the royal family, who, under the previous reign had been banished or degraded, were restored to their dignities and given the privilege of wearing that badge of close relationship, the yellow girdle.

ATTITUDE TOWARDS CHRISTIANITY. The hopes of the missionaries were at first high, but favorable expectations were not realized. The regents were hostile and the laws against the preaching of Christianity remained in force. In individual cases, however, favor was shown to the Jesuits, and two of their number, the painters and architects Castiglioni and Attiret, were employed for the purpose of building the royal palace and pavilions, and, incidentally, painting the royal countenance. The security of these artist priests was furthermore useful in obtaining favors for others. Further south the Christian teachers did not fare so well, and a terrible persecution broke out in the province of Fuh kien. A number of Spanish Dominicans were seized, tortured and decapitated, and the like fate was shared by a large number of their converts. Some excuse may possibly be urged for the reactionary feeling, in the light of the terrible massacres of Chinese which had recently taken place under the Spaniards in

the Philippines. After A. D. 1747 the missionaries were unmolested for a generation, but in
1784 a new inquisition was ordered through the
discovery that priests were still abroad in disguise.
Eighteen of these were captured, of whom six succumbed to the hardships of imprisonment, nine
left the country and three entered the service of
the Emperor. It is worth remembering that this
was "the last general crusade officially undertaken
against foreign propagandists."

REBELLION IN THE SOUTHWEST. Shortly after
the accession of Kien lung his mettle was tried by
a formidable rebellion which broke out in the
southwest provinces and extended to Hunan and
Kwang si. General Chang kwang was sent to the
seat of disturbance and prosecuted the campaign
with such success that the trouble was over in four
months. Unfortunately, the general was not able
to repeat his success when the aborigines of Sze
ch'uen, under Salopan, revolted in 1746. General Chang and a fellow-general quarreled, and in
consequence failed. The penalty of failure was
a polite invitation from the Emperor for each to
commit suicide, and the laurels of the new campaign were reaped by General Fu-ti, who was himself destined in later years to repeat the tragedy
of the famous soldier he had superseded. Solon's
aphorism "Let no man be called happy till his
death" is abundantly applicable to the great
names of China.

WARS IN CENTRAL ASIA. Yung chêng's policy

of retreat from Central Asia proved unfortunate and the reëstablishment of Chinese authority cost Kienlung an immense sacrifice of blood and treasure. The circumstances under which interference again became necessary are briefly as follows: The death of the Eleuth chief led to a contest for the succession between a son named Dardsha and a more distant relative Davatsi. The cause of the latter was espoused by the fickle and ambitious Amursana, who had regard mainly to his own profit. Dardsha was slain and then the allies fell out. Amursana fled to the Chinese court and under specious promises of allegiance obtained the support of the Emperor. Notwithstanding his pledge, he soon began to assume the airs of independent sovereignty, and, on being summoned to Peking, truculently prepared for war. Kien lung, too, made preparations, determined to hunt down his adversary "like a wolf," though the nobles of the court strongly advised him to leave Central Asia to its own dissensions. The campaign was planned by the Emperor to work out with the precision of a game of chess, but the plans miscarried for a time, and the Chinese statesmen were all the more anxious to give up the enterprise. Even Kienlung hesitated for a time. He soon, however, recovered his determination, and fortunately two generals were forthcoming who were equal to the task assigned them. These were the already famous Fu-ti and General Chao. The one was a Manchu and the other a

THE ELEUTHS PAY HOMAGE TO KIEN LUNG

Chinaman, but they worked well together, and before very long Amursana was a fugitive. He died of smallpox in Russian territory, and so great was Kienlung's desire to gloat over the corpse of his foe, or perhaps to make assurance doubly sure, that he insisted for a time on the body being forwarded to Peking. Fortunately, probably, for the health of the Emperor, the Russians proved stubborn. The victorious generals were received with almost royal honors and the Emperor went a day's journey to meet them. A curious light is thrown upon the ceremonialism of Chinese life by the story that after the death of Chao the Emperor still went to visit him. He had the body placed in a chair, dressed up as in life, and addressed the corpse with courteous solicitude, expressing the hope for a speedy recovery.

With the pacification of Kashgaria as *un fait accompli* Kienlung, leaving his "far-flung" frontier to the west as it had been in the glorious times of the Han and T'ang dynasties, was enabled to turn his attention to other problems.

"THE FLIGHT OF A TATAR TRIBE." One remarkable result of the improved conditions in Central Asia within the sphere of Chinese influence is seen in the return of the Turguts, a story so graphically described by De Quincy in an essay which has been termed by Dr. David Masson as a "noble effort of historical painting done with a sweep and breadth of poetic imagination entitling it, though a history, to rank also among his prose phantasies." The Turguts were a tribe which had settled across the Russian border on the banks of the Volga in order to escape the troubles caused by the ambitious projects of Galdan. Their new home pleased them after a while no better than the old, and when they heard of the new era of peace brought about by the conquests of Kienlung, their homesickness rendered intolerable the exactions of the Russian government and the laws as to conscription in which they had hitherto acquiesced. Thereupon commenced a migration almost without precedent in the world's history. A great multitude of men, women and children, numbering at least three hundred thousand souls, secretly set out to regain the old pasture lands of the tribes once again under the protection of the Emperors of China. It was at the beginning of January, A. D. 1771, that the horde started eastwards and not long after the Cossacks, apprised, like Pharaoh, of the flight from the land of a multitude of useful serfs, started after them and pursued them with fearful slaughter. Month after month, for eight months, the fugitives continued their journey, harassed by enemies and tortured by thirst, their ranks thinned continually by weariness and the length of the way. The worst experience came towards the end, when the Chinese cavalry sent by Kien lung was already approaching to relieve them. How the Bashkirs and Kirghizes of the desert swooped down upon them, how pursuers and pursued alike, slaughterers and slaughtered, alike tortured even to madness by thirst, came at last to Lake Tengis; how all continued to rush still slaying and being slain, into the water, till the lake was dyed and polluted with gore—all this must be read in the vivid account of De Quincy in order to realize it. Even while Turguts and Bashkirs were struggling together in frenzied hatred, came down the Chinese cavalry, and once again the slaughter, this time of the Bashkirs, raged, until the wild tribes of the desert were driven away to perish almost inevitably of thirst, "a retaliatory chastisement more complete and absolute than any which their swords and lances could have obtained, or human vengeance could have devised." The new subjects of the Empire were received with every demonstration of welcome, and next year a still further migration of some thirty thousand families followed the Turguts to enjoy the beneficent rule of Kienlung.

WAR IN BURMAH. In A. D. 1768 trouble arose with the kingdom of Ava or Burmah, and the Emperor handled the situation with his usual thoroughness. Raids across the border had long tried the patience of the Chinese governors, and fugitives, dissatisfied with the government on either side of the line, were only too ready to promote complications. Such complications, however, made it necessary to put an army in the field. Several notable victories were won by the

Chinese forces, and the Burmese commander so little distinguished himself that his master sent him a woman's dress to wear, as more suitable than the garb of a soldier. Ere long, however, the invaders, entangled in the land, found themselves in difficulties, and on one occasion the general had to order a *sauve qui peut*. If it had not been for the superior diplomacy of the Chinese, their valor in this campaign might have availed them little and the matter might have terminated disastrously. So well, however, did General Alikwan acquit himself as a diplomatist that he saved the situation, and Burmah was induced to enroll herself among the tribute-bearing nations. Every three years henceforward, the tokens of submission were sent to the court at Peking, and this was permitted even after the annexation of Burmah to Great Britain in 1886, out of a desire at that time not to open up new questions with China.

CONQUEST OF THE MIAO TSZ. We have already spoken of the hardy aboriginal race shut up in the mountains of Sze ch'uen, which from time to time was called upon to make such desperate efforts for independent existence. Kienlung was greatly desirous to reduce these brave mountaineers to submission, and the pretext of brigandage was as good as any other. The reduction was almost an extermination, for the Miao tsz made for the space of a year and a half, a desperate defense of their lives and homes. Even the women fought and every rock was defended to the last foothold.

In the end the last fortress was stormed and the captured chiefs were sent to Peking. The Emperor sullied ineffacably the glory of his victory by the murder of the men to whom, on their surrender, a guarantee of life had been given, and their heads, exposed in cages, spoke even more eloquently of the treachery of the Manchu than of the bravery of the victor. The victory was further commemorated by a monumental inscription, which is still to be seen under its yellow-tiled roof in front of the great Confucian Temple at Peking. The monumental tablets of Kien lung run as follows:

A. D. 1750. Kien lung. Conquest of the Miao country.

A. D. 1760. Kien lung. Conquest of Sungaria, the land of the Kalmucks.

A. D. 1760. Kien lung. Conquest of Muhamadan Tatary.

A. D. 1777. Kien lung. Conquest of the Miao country in Sze ch'uen.

The fortunate general Akwei was made a duke, whilst poor Fu ti, in spite of all his former services rendered to the state, suffered the fate of those who failed and was put to death.

WAR IN TIBET. A still further experience in campaigning was necessitated by the condition of affairs in Tibet. The circumstances leading up to this situation were these. The Panshen Lama died, whilst on a visit to Peking, of smallpox, and the Emperor undertook to send back his goods, which were of considerable value, to his elder brother. The body also was sent back, but Kienlung built a beautiful white marble monument over the clothes of the deceased. The carving on this strange memorial has been pronounced the most exquisitely beautiful of any in Peking. The younger surviving brother of the dead Lama had been excommunicated because of his attachment to the heterodox sect of "Red Caps," but he at once claimed the succession and called in the stalwart Himalayan tribesman known as Gurkhas to his support. A Chinese general who had been sent to drive out the marauders found it easier to use other weapons than those of war, and promised an annual bribe to the Gurkhas if they would retire and keep out of Tibet for the future. Unfortunately the wily diplomat provided no means for the fulfilment of his pledge, and left it to his successor to discover that such a pledge had been given. The discovery, as might have been expected, brought on war. The campaign was conducted with remarkable skill and success, and the Gurkhas were expelled. The Tibetans acknowledged themselves vassals of China and "from that day to this tribute missions, in compliance with this treaty, have without fail wended their weary way through the wastes of Tibet to Peking, at the stated intervals agreed upon." [1]

FORMOSA. The island of Tai wan, or Formosa, had always been a problem for the statesmen of China, and most rulers preferred to leave the island severely alone, or to see it in the occupation of another power. But a local chief named Lin had defeated a small Chinese force which had landed there, and, Kienlung's pride being at stake, an army of a hundred thousand men was dispatched to bring the troublesome dependency again under Chinese rule. The work was done, somewhat perhaps on the principle of making a desert and proclaiming peace. The victory provided the top-stone for Kienlung's pyramid of military fame. The Emperor, however, needed a summit higher than any of the mountains of China for the vantage point from which he could recite his poem:

> "Beneath my feet my realm I see
> As in a map unrolled."

THE MACARTNEY MISSION. The port of Canton had gradually become a storm center. The concentration of trade and traders in this vicinity both created and expressed the grievances which were more or less inseparable at this time from the presence of foreigners in China. In the year of Kien lung's accession there were at Canton four English, two French, two Dutch, one Danish and one Swedish vessel. In 1742 the first English warship arrived at Macao, and from that distance surveyed the situation. In 1759 Mr. Flint, from Ningpo, made his remarkable attempt to reach the august ear of the Emperor on the subject of commercial misunderstandings. The effort ended in his own banishment and in the decapitation of the Chinaman who had written the memorial. Then came, in A. D. 1784, the incident of the English gunner who had unintentionally killed a Chinaman whilst firing a salute. The unfortunate man was eventually surrendered to the Chinese authorities and strangled. So the causes for misunderstanding multiplied and the British government saw at length the need of dealing with the situation in order to protect honest trade and curb the lawlessness which was associated with that which was not honest. Captain Cathcart was first selected in 1788, but died on the outward journey. There was some inevitable delay, but in 1792 the Earl of Macartney arrived with a large suite and at once prepared for the visit to Peking. Of course, the Chinese could hardly appreciate the importance of intervention in a mere matter of trade. It was well-nigh unthinkable to the high officials at Peking that matters of state could be associated with commerce. Nevertheless, the Emperor was grateful for the moral support England had given in the affair of the Gurkhas, and Lord Macartney was most hospitably received. The Emperor entertained his visitors most lavishly, and it is estimated that $850,000 was spent on the various entertainments. Kien lung was also much interested in George Staunton, the ambassador's page, then only thirteen years old, and the only member of the Embassy familiar with the Chinese language.   Afterwards, as Sir George Staunton, this favored youth was able to write a most valuable account of the expedition. Lord Macartney had no reason to be displeased with his reception, but as an historian pertinently observes, "he did no business." Moreover, the Chinese had taken care to have painted on the sails of the vessel which carried the party up the river the words *"Tribute bearers from the country of England."* Consequently, in the eyes of the admiring natives, England too was numbered with the vassals. A competent writer observes of Lord Macartney's mission: "All he succeeded in exacting from the Government was a permission that his countrymen might trade at Canton on sufferance, as long as they obeyed the orders of the authorities."

The Dutch Mission. If the English had no reason to felicitate themselves upon the results of their mission, what are we to say of the mission of the Dutch in the following year? Van Braam, the Dutch agent at Canton, thought it possible to succeed where Lord Macartney had all but openly failed, but he really opened the door for humiliations such as no other body of Europeans ever consented to accept. The chief Commissioner was Isaac Titsingh, and his story is one of incredible servility. As Dr. Williams puts it, the ambassadors "were brought to the capital like malefactors, treated when there like beggars and sent back again to Canton like mountebanks." They were fed on broken meats served on dirty plates, and, when they returned to Canton in April, 1796, they had nothing upon which to look back except a record of insults on the one hand and obsequiousness on the other.

KIEN LUNG'S INTEREST IN LITERATURE. Kienlung, like the English Henry the Eighth, had been trained rather for scholarship than for a throne, and on attaining sovereignty kept his interest in literature. He earnestly labored for the perfecting of his mother tongue, the Manchu, and had many translations made of Chinese books. He took pains to have the Imperial eloquence perpetuated in monumental inscriptions, and in this way also, as we have seen, commemorated his victories in Central Asia and elsewhere. As a poet Kien lung is credited with 33,950 poems, in twenty-four volumes. These were written between 1736 and 1783, and while the substance is often sufficiently mediocre, the Emperor sometimes succeeded in attaining considerable originality of form. In one of his Manchu poems he used for the first, and possibly for the last, time verses which rhymed at the beginning as well as at the end of the lines. The best known of the royal poems are the *"Eulogy on Mukden"* and the verses on *Tea*. The former, in praise of the old capital of the Manchus, is a curiosity in more than one sense. It is written in Chinese and in Manchu. The Chinese version is a mass of recondite classical allusions and quotations, which make necessary the services of a very expert Chinese *literatus* to interpret. The Manchu version is as simple as the other is obscure. The poem, moreover, is written in sixty-four different scripts, of which thirty-two are genuine varieties of the Chinese character and thirty-two invented forms of *Manchu*, designed to correspond with the Chinese. The poem on *Tea* was composed in 1746, when the Emperor was hunting in Tatary, and no doubt well disposed towards the "cup that cheers." He had it inscribed on porcelain cups of a new sort, so that all who drank might read. Translated by Père Amiot, the poem found its way to Paris, where it attracted the attention of Voltaire. The French poet addressed a poetical epistle to the royal bard of China, which commences as follows:

"Recois mes compliments, charmant roi de la Chine;
Ton trône est donc placé sur la double colline!
On sait dans l' Occident que, malgré mes travers,
J'ai toujours fort aimé les rois qui fout des vers."

Professor Giles in his *"Chinese Literature"* gives a spirited translation of the song written by Kien lung for insertion in a play entitled *"Picking up Gold."* [2]

The French missionaries were not altogether without justification in placing beneath the portrait of Kien lung the words:

"Occupé sans relâche à tous les soins divers
D'un gouvernement qu'on admire,

Le plus grand potentat qui soit dans l'univers
Est le meilleur lettré qui soit dans son Empire."

FESTIVITIES. Kien lung was not, however, engaged all the time either in writing poems or in making war. His reign was marked by many great celebrations, and the older he got the more he delighted in opportunities for elaborate ceremony. As we have seen, he celebrated royally the return of the victorious generals from Central Asia.

In 1752 he observed the sixtieth birthday of the Empress Dowager with pageantry which filled seven miles of streets with wonderful sights,— sights, however, which were denied to the people all along the route. These had perforce to remain behind closed shutters and drawn curtains.

In 1761 he celebrated with great *éclat* his own fiftieth birthday, and took advantage of the occasion to receive formally the great geographical work of the Jesuit fathers, Benoit and Hallerstein. In 1767 he made an especially grand function of the plowing ceremony. Finally, he celebrated the attainment of his sixty year cycle, the goal of his desire from his earliest manhood, a goal granted to few monarchs to attain.

THE ABDICATION OF KIEN LUNG. With age comes sadness, and Kien lung was no exception. He had lost his mother, to whom he had always given the profoundest reverence, in 1777. The loss of his eldest son, in whom fine qualities had been discerned, followed soon after. The death of a trusted prime minister added a further blow. All this was an intimation to Kien lung that his own work was done. The primary reason, however, for his abdication was his unwillingness to trespass upon a cycle belonging to a successor, or to pass beyond the years of the reign of Kang hsi, his illustrious grandfather. The abdication took place quietly and Kien lung lived three years longer to watch over the early career of his successor. The reign thus brought to a voluntary close is unquestionably one of the greatest in all Chinese history and its successes were due quite as much to the genius of the Emperor as to his good fortune. He was indefatigable in his attention to business and often, at the age of eighty, rose in the middle of the night, however rigorous the season, for the holding of audiences, a practice which some of the missionaries and foreign ambassadors were honest enough to acknowledge inconvenient. He made great efforts to avert the mischief caused by the rising of the Hoang-ho, visited the southern provinces six times, was generous in the remission of taxes during periods of public calamity, and severe in his punishment of unfaithful officials. He was prejudiced against the Muhamadans of the northwestern provinces and is said to have contemplated at one time a general massacre. Nevertheless, he had a Muhamadan wife and loved her so well that he built for her a dwelling of two stories so arranged that she might face both the mosque across the street and her native Turkestan at one and the same time. Kien lung also took some measures, ineffectively, as it happened, for the suppression of the secret societies which had become especially troublesome about A. D. 1793. In the words of the Chinese proverb he "stirred the cane-brakes and roused the snake." From this half-measure his successor was destined to suffer severely.

NOTES

1. Douglas, "China," p. 171.
2. Giles, "Chinese Literature," p. 389.

CHAPTER VI

THE REIGN OF KIA KING

A. D. 1796—1820.

The reign of Kia king—the downfall of Ho shên—the rectitude of Sung—the Secret Societies—conspiracies against the Emperor—national calamities—"the Foam of the Sea"—the Opium question—the Amherst Mission—Robert Morrison—Thomas Manning—death of the Emperor.

The Reign of Kia king. The Ta' Ts'ing dynasty forms no exception to the general rule, which finds such frequent exemplification in the dynastic history of China, that the strong men fought for and maintained the Empire whilst the weak ones brought it to the verge of ruin. The first century and a half of Manchu rule was a period of ever increasing glory and success; the last century was an era of disaster during which the thread suspending the sword of Damocles was wearing ever thinner. A prediction respecting the dynasty ran somewhat as follows:

"Over the land of peace and rest trouble rises like the tide; and the year sixteen demands that we prepare on every side. Now await the coming years of Lungshay and stalking Ma, when five nations will convulse our flowery land." Whatever be the astronomical conjunction here designated, the time of trouble was now at hand and largely through the "five" nations, taking five in its Chinese sense of the perfect number. Almost all our information as to the reign must necessarily be derived from outside sources, since the dynastic history of the Manchus has yet to be published. M. Rémusat speaks of the *Tung hwa lu* ("Chronicle of the Eastern Flower"), a work in manuscript in sixteen volumes, as the sole Chinese written authority for the history as late as the reign of Kia king. Fortunately, the time is sufficiently near our own to obtain some idea of its general character. Moreover, the record is a somewhat dismal one, the record of a time whose troubles were fitly enough presaged by the appearance of a great comet, or "broom-tailed star," which hung, we are told menacingly in the heavens for twelve months from the time of Kia king's accession. Beneath that menace Kia king, "churlish, sordid and uncouth," begirt himself for the stupendous task of government bequeathed to him by his illustrious ancestors.

THE DOWNFALL OF HO SHÊN. A serious loss sustained by the new sovereign soon after his assumption of power was that of the great Manchu minister Ho shên. He had risen from a very humble station and had attracted the notice of Kien lung because of his good looks whilst acting as a guard at the palace gates. Happily he had other qualities in addition to his good looks, and ere the end of Kien lung's reign had become almost what Cardinal Wolsey was to Henry VIII. Like Wolsey, too, he had his fall, though not till the accession of a new monarch. Too powerful to be at once assailed, Ho shên found his position gradually sapped and undermined by his detractors, and his appointment as superintendent of the obsequies of Kien lung gave opportunity enough for charges of corruption. Sixteen articles of impeachment were drawn up, most of them frivolous enough, but there was sufficient evidence of his self-enrichment to condemn him, and he was graciously permitted to be his own executioner. His private fortune which was estimated at the huge figure of $105,000,000, was confiscated.

The Rectitude of Sung. Another famous statesman was, with all his ups and downs, more fortunate. This was Sung Yün, who had risen from a petty government clerkship to membership in the Great Council. In this capacity he was chosen to accompany Lord Macartney on his "tribute bearing" mission to Peking. He acted throughout with great tact and had the unusual luck to please both sides. His acceptance, however, of presents from the English in recognition of his courtesy whilst engaged as escort, drew upon him the anger of his government. The presents were returned and he was degraded.

Further trouble came through his outspoken remonstrances with the Emperor. With great courage Sung presented himself before His Majesty and upbraided him with his vicious and extravagant life, spent rather with actors than with men of dignity and learning. The Chinese ruler was no more pleased than was Herod with John the Baptist and indignantly asked what punishment was due to a man guilty of such audacity. Sung replied quite coolly, "Quartering." Asked to name another mode of death a trifle less dishonorable, the minister replied, "Beheading." Still again interrogated, he answered, "Strangling." By this time the Emperor's wrath was mollified and Sung obtained the applause due to his rectitude. Nevertheless, lest he should approach his sovereign too frequently with ill-timed remonstrances, he was sent away to Mongolia. Vicissitudes of fortune continued, and by A. D. 1819 the once powerful Censor had been reduced to a mere lieutenancy among the bannermen. Then in 1820, when Kia king's funeral was being celebrated in Peking, the new Emperor, Tao kwang, following his father's coffin between long lines of officials, suddenly caught sight of the unfortunate Sung standing humbly in the throng. He went aside and embraced him, weeping, and soon after restored him to rank and to the governorship of Jehol. From that time onwards Sung lived prosperously until his death in 1835.

THE SECRET SOCIETIES. The entire reign of Kia king was disturbed by the agitations of the various secret societies. This was especially the case in the south. The whole valley of the Si Kiang was a center of intense political and religious unrest for many years. The government maintained the greatest severity against the White Lotus, the Triads, the Society of Heavenly Reason and such like orders, but without much result. In 1801 the throne decreed the summary execution of all members of the societies engaged in pillage. In 1810 the people of Fuh kien were warned that if they favored the Triad movement the severest penalties would be visited upon them. The Government measures in this direction cost, we are told, the sum of 100,000,000 taels, and in one province alone twenty or thirty thousand persons are said to have been executed. Ten thousand condemned criminals were in the prisons at one time and so great was the fear of the Government that meetings of more than five persons were proclaimed as seditious.

CONSPIRACIES AGAINST THE EMPEROR. In two conspiracies organized by the secret societies the Emperor nearly lost his life. The first was in 1803, when many persons in high estate, including even relatives of the Emperor, were involved. Even more keen than the dagger of the assassin was to the sovereign the indifference with which the whole affair was regarded at court and in the country. It rankled deeply that hardly anyone rallied to the sovereign's side. "It is this indifference," he said, "rather than the poignard of the assassin which hurts me most." The conspiracy of 1813 was more serious still. An insurrection organized by the Heavenly Reason and White Lotus Societies broke out in Ho-nan and Chih li; many cities were taken by storm and in broad daylight a party of conspirators entered the royal palace and fought body to body with the guards. The Emperor coming out was seized by the throat and it would have gone hard with him had not the prince Mien ning (the future Emperor Tao kwang) shot two of the assailants with a matchlock. A third was slain by a nephew (or cousin) and by this time the soldiers arrived. For his valor on this occasion the prince Mien ning was nominated heir to the throne.

NATIONAL CALAMITIES. The unrest of the populace is only too easy to understand when we have our attention drawn to the terrible devastation of the land by hurricane and flood, especially when we remember the intimate connection the Chinese have always perceived between physical disasters and bad government. The great drought of 1817 caused the Board of Punishments to consult together as to whether they had been properly fulfilling their duties. They drew up a document in which the hope was expressed that Nature would soon reëstablish her proper order. The Emperor himself, in acordance with the old customs, was moved to self-examination and confession of sins for himself and for his people. Some sentences are worth quoting: "The remissness and sloth of the officers of government constitute an evil which has long been accumulating. It is not the evil of a day; for several years I have given the most pressing admonitions on the subject, and have punished many cases which have been discovered, so that recently there appears a little improvement and for several seasons the weather has been favorable. The drought this season is perhaps not entirely on this account. I have meditated upon it and am persuaded that the reason why the azure Heavens above manifested disapprobation by withholding rain for a few hundred miles only around the capital, is that the fifty and more rebels who escaped are secreted somewhere near Peking. Hence it is that fertile vapors are fastbound and the felicitous harmony of the seasons interrupted." [1] In spite of all this, storms and floods followed upon the drought, and the only reason the perplexed Emperor could assign for the visitation was that perhaps, since the storms had come from the southeast, there were officials in that direction who had "excited the ire of heaven."

"THE FOAM OF THE SEA." In addition to the sufferings entailed by the rise of the secret societies and the convulsions of unquiet Nature, were those brought upon the southern provinces by the pirates. The estuary of the Si Kiang has always enjoyed the sinister reputation of being the most pirate-infested water in the world. Even now merchantmen at times require an escort and the exposure of pirates' heads in baskets, or the bricking up of pirates in chimneys, has so far failed to deter these rovers of the sea from the pursuit of their calling. Kia king's reign furnished unlimited opportunity for the display of their daring. Under two adventurous leaders, Ching Yih and Chang Pau, six hundred junks ravaged the coasts of Kwangtung for several years and made the Pearl River so dangerous that the Governor of Canton himself transferred his residence to Macao. In the course of these years two Englishmen, Messrs. Turner and Glaspoole, were made prisoners and their capture proved in part the undoing of the sea robbers. For the prisoners utilized their enforced leisure to learn a good deal respecting the organization of the pirates which they were able subsequently to turn to good account. Eventually the two chiefs were alienated and the government succeeded in taking advantage of the quarrel. The assistance of the English was also invoked on the occasion of the coming of the Siamese tribute by sea. This was a prize eagerly awaited by the robbers, but the ship *Mercury* scattered them most effectually and for once the foreigners earned the gratitude of the Chinese officials. "The story of those disturbed times," says Dr. Wells Williams, "to this day affords a frequent subject for the tales of old people in that region and the same waters are still infested by 'the foam of the sea,' as the Chinese term these freebooters."

THE OPIUM QUESTION. As though the questions already at issue between the merchants trading at Canton and the Provincial and National Governments were not sufficiently bristling with difficulties, another question now arose in an acute form for the first time. This was the question as to the trade in opium. The poppy, according to Dr. Edkins, is mentioned in Chinese books as far back as the Eighth Century. It was probably introduced by the Arabs and prized originally for its flowers which were esteemed by the Chinese next to those of the peony. Later on, the medicinal properties of the poppy were discovered, but it was probably not till the introduction of tobacco from the Philippines in A. D. 1620 that the habit of smoking opium commenced. The earliest practice was to mix some portion of the opium with the tobacco. The vicious habit became noticeable first in Amoy, which was the port of entry for Manila, and in Formosa. A book of the time, quoted by Edkins, describes the ill effects which were perceived. "Depraved young men without any fixed occupation used to meet together by night to smoke: it grew to be a custom with them. . . . In order to tempt new smokers to come, no charge was made the first time. After some time they could not stay away and could come even if they forfeited all their property.   Smokers were able to remain awake the whole night, and rejoiced as an aid to sensual indulgence.   Afterwards they found themselves beyond the possibility of cure. . . . It is truly sad to reflect on this."   Edicts prohibiting the trade were issued from A. D. 1729 onwards but the efforts made to stamp it out though undoubtedly sincere, were without avail.   The traffic remained in Portuguese hands till 1773 when Clive's conquest of Bengal led to the association of the East India Company with the unhappy business.   With a curious casuistry the Company manufactured the drug in India expressly for Chinese consumption but, on their attention being drawn to the pernicious effects of opium smoking, they gave orders that no ships belonging to the Company should take any to China.   After the close of the Eighteenth Century, says Capt. Brinkley, "they never carried an ounce of it in their own vessels."   The responsibility for the demoralizing situation created must be shared by the East India Company with the smugglers who defied all law, foreign and Chinese alike, first from Macao and later from Lintin; with the *hong* merchants who evaded all regulations for restricting the sale of the drug, and with the Chinese officials who were themselves frequently the slaves of the habit and at least disposed to make illegitimate profit by its introduction.   This connivance rendered all the edicts issued from Peking futile and even farcical.

THE AMHERST MISSION. Foreign relations were unsatisfactory throughout the reign of Kia king. He was himself personally antipathetic to foreigners, as may be seen by the single episode of his expulsion of Père Amiot, after the latter had resided in Peking for thirty years. Still, apart from the opium question, the relation of foreign nations to China was provocative and vexatious. War was proceeding between France and England and the parties to the conflict seemed to consider Chinese territory as a kind of "Tom Tiddler's ground." At least that is the only interpretation we can give to the fact that in spite of the Chinese claim to sovereignty in Macao (leased to Portugal), England seized the place in 1802 to prevent its being seized by France and repeated the occupation in 1808. Later, the war with America took place and English cruisers played hide-and-seek with American merchantmen in Chinese waters without scruple. This almost inevitably led to protests on the part of China and, when these were ineffectual, to interference with English trade in Canton. Then the necessity of supplying the teacups of England with the national beverage led to the suggestion of another Mission, modeled after that of Lord Macartney. This was headed by Lord Amherst, who had formerly been Governor General of India. The party included as interpreter the famous missionary, Robert Morrison, and the picturesque traveler, Thomas Manning. It started for Peking in 1816 and reached the capital on August 28. Impartial historians have summed up the result in one pregnant word, "mismanagement." Others have talked about the "ignorance, pride, isolation and audacity" of the Chinese. The truth is that the mandarins of the court did not want the mission to succeed, and took no pains to apprise the Emperor of the situation. The Emperor himself was not necessarily to blame for fixing the hour of the interview at a time inconvenient to Lord Amherst. Chinese sovereigns were accustomed to giving audiences at unearthly hours, and it probably did not occur to Kia king that he was insulting his guest by asking him to appear immediately on arrival and before his uniform had arrived. Possibly Lord Amherst, who had for a time held out against Manning as interpreter because he deemed the latter's flowing beard "incongruous," was over-fastidious in his insistence on the niceties of diplomatic etiquette. At this distance it seems a pity that the whole mission should have failed because of differences of this kind. In any case, insistence on punctilio rendered the accomplishment of any results through the mission impossible. It retired without effecting even an interview with majesty. A valuable opportunity for promoting mutual understanding was missed, and, indeed, extra reasons for misunderstanding accumulated. The Emperor visited with severe penalties, when it was too late, the obstructive mandarins, but possibly these had not very seriously misinterpreted the Emperor's own feelings towards the foreigners. At least his letter addressed at an earlier period to King George III begins with this sentence: "Your Majesty's kingdom is at a remote distance beyond the seas, but is observant of its duties and obedient to our laws, beholding from afar the glory of our Empire and respectfully admiring the perfection of our government." The letter ends with this other sentence, a very polite way of saying, "Ambassadors not wanted": "With regard to those of your Majesty's subjects who for a long course of years have been in the habit of trading with our Empire, we must observe to you that our Celestial Government regards all persons and nations with eyes of charity and benevolence, and always treats and considers your subjects with the utmost indulgence and affection; on their account, therefore, there can be no place or occasion for the exertions of Your Majesty's Government." A somewhat similar rebuff was given to Russia in 1805.

ROBERT MORRISON. More than one foreigner at this epoch has a rightful place in a history of China, by the testimony of the Chinese themselves and out of recognition of the place they occupied whilst alive and the influence they were destined to exert after death. One of these is assuredly the great pioneer missionary, Robert Morrison, who was accepted for service in China in 1805 by the London Missionary Society and commenced forthwith that devoted study of the language which has made his labors so useful to so many successors. He arrived in China in 1807, after two years' study of Chinese manuscripts in the British Museum, and in 1809 was appointed translator to the East India Company. It is a curious sign of the timidity with which missionary work was at this time approached that when the Directors of the East India Company learned that Morrison was the author of religious tracts, they ordered his dismissal, fearing that Chinese prejudice would be aroused against the Company. Fortunately the agents on the spot had come to know Morrison's value and secured the retention of his services. There is no space here for an account of the labors of Morrison as missionary and as translator. Suffice it to say that Professor Julien describes the "*Dictionary of the Chinese Language*" as "without dispute the best Chinese dictionary composed in a European language." Morrison died in 1834 and was buried at Macao, where he shares with Camoens the pleasanter associations of the place.

THOMAS MANNING. Less prominent, but still worthy of mention is Manning, who is indirectly known to all readers of Charles Lamb's "*Dissertation on Roast Pig*," and its reference to a certain Chinese manuscript which "my friend M. was obliging enough to read and explain to me." Manning studied Chinese at Cambridge and Paris and was by some regarded as the first Chinese scholar in Europe. He went out to Canton as a physician in 1807 and made several attempts to reach the interior of China. His travels in Tibet, and how he became the first white visitor to the forbidden city of Lhassa are mentioned by the Abbé Huc. His position as junior secretary with Lord Amherst's expedition has already been alluded to. But in truth a romantic career such as that of Manning cannot be dealt with in a paragraph. Our last impression of him is as living in a large unfurnished house in England with "a vast library of Chinese books" and a roomful of visitors drawn together by his delightful conversation. He died in 1840 and was buried in the abbey at Bath.

DEATH OF KIA KING. The Emperor, whose excessive devotion to pleasure had for a long while made him a subject for animadversion, if not an object of contempt, to the best minds of China, died on September 2, 1820, at the age of sixty-one and after a troubled reign of twenty-five years. His will, which has been translated by Morrison, left the throne to his second son, Mien ning, known as the Emperor Tao kwang.

NOTE

1. S. Wells Williams, "Middle Kingdom," I, p. 465.

CHAPTER VII

THE REIGN OF TAO KWANG

A. D. 1820-1850.

*Tao kwang—the Edicts of Tao kwang—polit-
ical troubles—events in Canton—War with Great
Britain—the Treaty of Nanking and its results
—the situation at Canton—death of Tao kwang.*

TAO KWANG. Such was the name assumed by
the Prince Mien ning who had, as we have seen,
earned the gratitude of his father and the more
dubious heritage of the Dragon Throne by his
gallant defense of Kia king against the conspirators of 1813. He was regarded by those who knew
him as naturally rather stupid or else very unnaturally reserved. It really seems that he suffered
considerable deterioration as time went on. This
may have been the result of the various quacker-
ies with which he is said to have experimented in
order to increase his physical strength. These,
we are told, left him eventually toothless and hol-
low-cheeked. He is described as tall, lank and
dark-complexioned. Yet he had evidently more
character than his father, and could display on
occasion a resolution which his detractors might

even regard as obstinacy. He was probably sincere enough in his early efforts to cleanse the Augean stable of the court and may well have grown discouraged at the apparent futility of the task. Thence he sank into habits of debauchery which sadly disappointed the hopes which a creditable beginning had inspired. His life, moreover, was saddened by family troubles. One of his sons was a scapegrace and reprobate, devoted to the use of opium, and the Emperor is said to have slain him with a blow struck in a moment of uncontrollable anger—a moment vainly regretted forever after.

THE EDICTS OF TAO KWANG. We should probably be seriously misled if we formed our ideas of Chinese history from the Imperial Edicts, yet they now and then throw a good deal of light on the condition of affairs in China, as viewed from the Court point of view. We are compelled to say so much in these chapters of foreign affairs that it is not unfitting to quote from some of the Edicts of Tao kwang, as translated by Dr. Wells Williams.

1. In his first edict the Emperor refers to his deceased father in the following terms:—

"His late Majesty who has now gone the great journey, governed all under Heaven's canopy twenty-five years, exercising the utmost caution and industry. Nor evening nor morning was he ever idle. He assiduously aimed at the best possible rule and hence his government was illustrious and excellent; the court and the country felt the deepest reverence and the stillness of profound awe. . . . But in the midst of a hope that this glorious reign would be long protracted and the help of Heaven would be received many days, unexpectedly, on descending to bless by His Majesty's presence, Lwan yang the dragon charioteer, became a guest on high . . . My sacred and indulgent Father had, in the year that he began to rule alone, silently settled that the divine utensil should devolve on my contemptible person. I, knowing the feebleness of my virtue, at first felt much afraid I should not be competent to the office; but on reflecting that the sages, my ancestors, have left to posterity their plans; that His late Majesty has laid the duty on me—and Heaven's throne should not be long vacant—I have done violence to my feelings . . . and on the 27th of the eighth moon I purpose devoutly to announce the event to Heaven, to Earth, to my ancestors and to the gods of the land and the grain, and shall then sit down on the Imperial Throne." [1]

2. A second extract refers to the great drought of 1832. After various efforts to turn aside the wrath and conciliate the favor of Heaven, the Emperor published a memorial of which the following is an extract:

"Summer is past and no rain has fallen. Not only do agriculture and human beings feel the dire calamity, but also beasts and insects, herbs and trees, almost cease to live. I, the minister of Heaven, am placed over mankind and am responsible for keeping the world in order and tranquillizing the people. Although it is now impossible for me to sleep or eat with composure, although I am scorched with grief and tremble with anxiety, still, after all, no genial and copious showers have been obtained."

The Emperor proceeds to acknowledge: "The sole cause is the daily deeper atrocity of my sins; but little sincerity and little devotion. Hence I have been unable to move Heaven's heart and bring down abundant blessings." Then follows a detailed self-examination in which the monarch asks himself the most heart-searching questions. He concludes: "Prostrate I beg Imperial Heaven to pardon my ignorance and stupidity and to grant me self-renovation; for myriads of innocent people are involved by me, the One Man. My sins are so numerous it is difficult to escape from them. Summer is passed and autumn arrived." [2]

3. A third edict still may be quoted, this time issued for the purpose of bestowing honor upon the widow of Kia king on the attainment of her sixtieth birthday. It runs in part as follows:—

"In the first month of the present winter occurs the sixtieth anniversary of her Majesty's sacred natal day. At the opening of the happy period, the sun and the moon shed their united genial influences upon it. When commencing anew the revolution of the sexagenary cycle, the honor thereof adds increase to her felicity. Looking upwards and beholding her glory, we repeat our gratulations and announce the event to Heaven, to Earth, to our ancestors and to the patron gods of the Empire." [3]

POLITICAL TROUBLES. In spite of all these high-flown felicitations, the Empire was, during the reign of Tao kwang, rarely free from political trouble of one kind or another. The first uprising was in Turkestan in the neighborhood of Kashgar, about 1825. It was suspected from what was to be seen of the administration of the Chinese governors that the virility which had characterized the spacious times of Kanghsi and Kienlung was a thing of the past. Under the impulse of some such instinct, or in obedience to their own restless moods, the tribes rallied around one Jehanger, a descendant of the old chiefs or Khojans, and the Chinese garrison was massacred. A large army was immediately despatched, and after an exasperating and protracted campaign, which cost the government some ten million ounces of silver, Jehanger was captured and sent to Peking. Here he expiated his failure by suffering a cruel and lingering death.

The rebellion in *Formosa* and *Hainan* was less formidable and was put down by the use of bribery as much as by the sword. It is perhaps a mistake to speak of the rebellions in Formosa as ever being really suppressed, since no attempt was made to follow up the crushing of an insurrection by such a constructive policy as might ensure lasting tranquillity.

More serious was the new outbreak among the *Miao-tsze* of three provinces in 1832. These had suffered cruel exactions at the hands of the lawless bands belonging to the secret societies, and avenged themselves by the slaughter of the impotent and indifferent officials. They were then attacked in force. Choosing for their leader the chief known as the Golden Dragon, the tribesmen prepared energetically to defend themselves. The Chinese forces were at first under the Viceroy of Kwang tung, General Li, but his incompetence and cruelty led to his recall and Tao Kwang then sent his father-in-law to continue the campaign. Contrary to the general expectation, and possibly also to his deserts, Heng nan succeeded in putting an end to the revolt in ten days. It is said that considerable success attended a kind of "poster campaign" through which the people were graciously advised to return peaceably to their homes.

EVENTS IN CANTON. The real storm center of the Empire, however, was undoubtedly at Canton. In the space at our disposal it is impossible to do much more than to state the more salient facts as fairly and dispassionately as possible.[4] Judgment will probably follow racial or national feeling and it is as proper to assume the patriotism of Tao kwang and Commissioner Lin on the one hand as that of Lord Napier and Captain Elliott on the other. Circumstances being what they were and the limitations of human beings what they were, the result was almost bound to be what it was. It is our place to see to it that the difficulties dissipated with the battle-smoke of 1840 and subsequent years should no longer obstruct the mutual good relations between nations. The excuses that Chinese and English had for misunderstanding one another then are in no sense valid for us to-day. The fact that the difficulties at Canton were increasing with time and that the day was drawing near for the charter of the East India Company to expire prompted the British Government to prepare the way for a new order of things which, it was hoped, would be more satisfactory than the old. The old method was for the foreign merchants to be represented by a body called the *Tai pan*, the Chinese by the *Co hong*, and for the Chinese trade authorities to be the Viceroy of Kwangtung and an official from Peking known as the Hoppo. The plan, so far as it worked at all, worked on a basis of mutual arrangement and compromise. The new plan adopted by England was for a Commissioner to be appointed who should represent not the merchants merely, but the Government, and who should have *diplomatic* relations with the Chinese Government. In the commission forwarded to Lord Napier (the first appointee) by King George the Fourth, dated December 10, 1833, the objects were clearly enough stated. The Commissioner was expected to foster and protect trade at Can-

ton, to extend trade wherever possible in other
directions, and to open up direct communication
with Peking. The mistake was, however, made
of sending no real notice of the appointment to
China, of failing to make clear the relation of
Lord Napier to the Government rather than to
the merchants, and of overlooking the inability
of the Commissioner to control other nations
than his own, let alone the smugglers of all nations. So when, with the expiration of the charter of the East India Company, Lord Napier
commenced his task, there was not the smallest
likelihood that he would be able to carry it to a
successful conclusion. To begin with, it was impossible to open up communications with the Viceroy except through the *hong*. There is an element even of burlesque, if one were not sensible
of the terrible strain imposed by the proceedings upon the Commissioner, in the bandying to
and forth of missives such as those from which
we quote. Here is a characteristic bit of epis-
tolary conceit from the Governor: "To sum up
the whole matter, the nation has its laws. Even
England has its laws. How much more the Celestial Empire! How flaming bright are its
great laws and ordinances! More terrible than
the awful thunderbolts! Under this whole bright
heaven none dares to disobey them. Under its
shelter are the four seas. Subject to its sooth-
ing care are ten thousand kingdoms. The said
barbarian eye (Lord Napier) having come over

a sea of several myriads of miles in extent to examine and have superintendence of affairs, must be a man thoroughly acquainted with the principles of high dignity." [5]

And not altogether unlike is the letter from the Commissioner which concludes as follows: "I must now request you to declare to them (the Hong merchants) that His Majesty, the King of England, is a great and powerful monarch, that he rules over an extent of territory in the four quarters of the world more comprehensive in space and infinitely more so in power than the whole Empire of China, that he commands armies of bold and fierce soldiers who have conquered wherever they went; and that he is possessed of great ships where no native of China has ever yet dared to show his face. Let the Governor then judge if such a monarch will be 'reverently obedient' to anyone." [6]

It is not to be greatly wondered at that, while much of the trade went on as usual, the poor Commissioner, buffeted by many unexpected rebuffs, caught a fever from which he died at Macao on Oct. 11, 1834.

The *impasse* was unbroken when Captain Elliott (afterwards Sir Charles Elliott) arrived in 1836. Again the attempt was made to correspond directly with the Viceroy. Again His Excellency refused to accept any document unless it were headed with the word *p'in* or "*petition*." Elliott's dignity balked at this, although he yielded sufficiently to address letters through the Hoppo. So the situation continued. Then a new element was introduced from Peking. The grandees at the Imperial Court were by no means at one as to the policy to be pursued. There were two parties in the palace, one, headed by the Empress, favorable to the legalization of the trade in opium; another, headed by the Emperor, demanding total prohibition of the drug. The latter party naturally won in the contest of policy and the triumph produced speedy and spectacular results at Canton. Captain Elliott was no friend of the opium business, but he nevertheless believed sincerely that the best way of controlling the traffic was by legalization. His position was influenced, moreover, by some justifiable doubts as to the *bona fides* of the Chinese endeavor to abolish the traffic. Many officials were openly in connivance with the smugglers and the son of the obstinate Viceroy himself was profitably engaged in the business. The cultivation of the poppy was likewise increasing rapidly throughout the provinces, and the trade in the opium was to all appearances nowhere being interfered with except in Canton.

Matters were brought to a head by the appointment of *Lin Tsze su* as Imperial Commissioner. Few will question the genuine patriotism of this great Chinaman, though many will feel that he was *doctrinaire* and impetuous beyond the limits of good judgment. Born in A. D. 1785 in the province of Fuh Kien, he had risen to the position of Censor and thence to that of Governor of Hu Kuang. He was gazetted Imperial Commissioner in 1838 and Viceroy in 1839, arriving at his post on March 10 of the latter year. Things at once began to move, though unfortunately, in the direction of war. Lin demanded the surrender of all the opium in the hands of the merchants. These, not as yet knowing the man with whom they had to deal, subscribed something over a thousand chests as "a sop to Cerberus." Lin knew enough not to be satisfied with this, and at once ordered a siege of the foreign settlement until the last ounce should have been delivered up. This was a serious situation, and Captain Elliott saw no way out of it except to ask in the name of the British Government that the merchants should obey the peremptory demand. In a very short time 20,283 [7] chests were forthcoming, but Commissioner Lin would not raise the siege till the last particle was actually in his hands. All this entailed some forty-eight days' confinement of the foreign community, but Lin had gained his point. The whole of the drug was most effectually destroyed, and the Chinese counterpart of the "Boston Tea Party" might have done much to clear up the situation had not Lin confused the issues by other demands, such as that certain Europeans should be surrendered for punishment on account of alleged crimes on Chinese soil. These demands naturally were refused point blank, whilst the opium business, stimulated by the clearing out of the entire market, soon began to flourish anew, with raised prices and a brisk demand. Then occurred the arrival of two British warships and, in the tension of feeling then prevailing, it is not surprising that occasion was soon found for the naval engagement at Chuan pu on Nov. 3, 1839, by which several Chinese junks were destroyed. The whole lamentable dispute was thus for the time being transferred from the field of diplomacy to the bloody arbitrament of war.

War with Great Britain. "It was the closing of trade," says the Chinese historian Wei Yuan, "not the forced surrender of the opium, which brought on the Canton war." It is unfortunate indeed that the opening of China to the commerce of the western world was attended by war, and especially a war which was undertaken in connection with a traffic so iniquitous as that which dealt in opium. But it is difficult to apportion the blame justly between the two combatants and, once again, we must be content to recite the facts and take to heart the lessons. The first war with Great Britain was a somewhat desultory campaign. It was, moreover, carried on with a surprisingly small force on the English side, not more than nine thousand men being engaged at any one time, and the great city of Canton being stormed by a force of only five thousand effectives.

Only two ships were engaged in the affair at

Chuan pu, but by the end of June, 1840, there were seventeen men-of-war and twenty-seven troopships with four thousand soldiers at Hongkong. Canton was blockaded and Ting tai, on the island of Chusan, captured by Sir Gordon Bremer. Then the fleet sailed northwards from Ningpo to Taku at the mouth of the Pei ho. Here Captain Elliott was met by the Governor of Chih li, Ki shên, a diplomat whose career up to this time had been one long series of successes, but who from this time onward had much reason to regret his entanglement with the Empire's foreign affairs. Ki shên managed to persuade the fleet to return to Canton, where, meanwhile, things had gone from bad to worse. Poor Lin had now incurred the displeasure of the Emperor, who sent him word that he was "no better than a block of wood" and ordered him, nevertheless, to return to Peking, "with the speed of flames." Sir Gordon Bremer, returning to Canton, found nothing better to do than capture a few of the forts. This led Ki shên, now occupying Lin's former position, to suggest negotiations, and a convention was drawn up, known subsequently as the *Treaty of the Bogue*, by which Hongkong was ceded to Great Britain and an indemnity of six million dollars promised, to pay for the opium which had been destroyed. All this, however, was arranged independently of Peking, and the Emperor, so far from ratifying the instrument, sent more troops and peremptory orders to destroy the foreigners utterly, "and wash them clean away." As Ki shên failed to do this, he in turn was recalled. Then the war was resumed. The Bogue forts were captured, and the Imperial troops continued to assemble until there were in the neighborhood of Canton some fifty thousand Chinese soldiers, more or less equipped for war. Then a night attack was made on the British fleet and failed, and matters once again came to a halt. This unsatisfactory condition of affairs was relieved by the sending of Sir Henry Pottinger to take the place of Captain Elliott and the appointment of Sir Hugh Gough and Sir William Parker in charge respectively of the military and naval forces of Great Britain.

A vigorous campaign was at once initiated. Without any waste of time the expedition started northward, took the city of Amoy, retook Tingtai on the island of Chusan, and then in succession captured the cities of Chên hai, Ning po, Wu sung, Shanghai and Chên kiang. In some cities the Manchu garrisons made a very creditable defense; in others deplorable incidents took place, such as the suicide of some thousands of panic-stricken people at Chên kiang. Meanwhile the Commissioners Ilipu and Ki ying were despatched from Peking, and when Nanking, the old capital, was threatened, they appeared on the scene and associating with themselves another diplomat, one Niu kien, opened up communications with Sir Henry Pottinger. The negotiations this time went through satisfactorily, and on Aug. 29, 1842 there was signed on board H. M. S. *Cornwallis* the *Treaty of Nanking*, which Dr. Wells Williams has described as "one of the turning points in the history of mankind, involving the welfare of all nations in its wide-reaching consequences." It consisted of thirteen articles, of which the principal provisions arranged for the transfer of Hongkong to the British crown; the payment of $21,000,000 indemnity (made up of $6,000,000 for the opium, $3,000,000 for debts due to British subjects, and $12,000,000 for the expenses of the campaign); the opening, in addition to Canton, of the four ports of Amoy, Fuchow, Ningpo and Shanghai; and the recognition of the principle of extra-territoriality. So anxious were the authorities to see the last of the foreign ships that the treaty was hurried to Peking and returned signed with unusual celerity. By October the fleet had retired to Chusan, which it was decided to hold until the indemnity had been paid.

RESULTS OF THE TREATY OF NANKING. The results of the treaty of 1842 were far-reaching. Not only were the trade interests of Great Britain advanced through the possession of Hongkong (an island destined soon to become the greatest emporium in the East and the world's third largest port), but the other nations of Europe and America soon recognized the door opened for their own commerce. At last the walls of brass were broken down. Agents from Belgium, Holland, Spain, Prussia and Portugal appeared to measure the extent of their opportunities. Ministers extraordinary were appointed by France and the United States. President Taylor sent Mr. Caleb Cushing with a letter which has been much criticised for its "patronizing superiority," but which was really only an attempt to translate the President's thoughts into what he believed to be the appropriate verbiage of the Orient. It begins with an interesting little lesson in geography: "I hope your health is good. China is a great empire, extending over a great part of the world. The Chinese are numerous. You have millions and millions of subjects. The twenty-six United States are as large as China, though our people are not so numerous. The rising sun looks upon the great mountains and great rivers of China. When he sets he looks upon rivers and mountains equally large in the United States. Our territories extend from one great ocean to the other; and on the west we are divided from your dominions only by the sea. Leaving the mouth of one of our great rivers, and going constantly towards the setting sun, we sail to Japan and to the Yellow Sea." Mr. Cushing, nevertheless, arranged a treaty which was signed July 3, 1844, and cleared up matters so far as America was concerned. In one respect it went further, namely, in securing the right to the free exercise of the Christian religion in the open ports. "This right," says Lord William Cecil,[8] "sufficiently remarkable in itself, has often been stipulated by a State for its own nationals resident in a foreign country, but I doubt if it has ever before been known for a country to insist on the right of preaching a religion to somebody else's citizens." A French treaty was signed October 24 of the same year. Thus all the advantages which England had won by war were appropriated peacefully by the other powers. The one question which had, at least indirectly, been instrumental in bringing on the war was the one which remained totally unaffected by the various agreements. Opium was not placed among the dutiable articles. Efforts were indeed made to have the traffic legalized, and so controlled, but without result.

THE SITUATION AT CANTON. The signing of the treaty of peace at Nanking had little or no effect in pacifying Canton. It is not creditable to the reputation of foreigners that in the city where they had lived the longest and were presumably best known, they were least liked. The law of extra-territoriality was particularly resented, and difficult to enforce. In 1847 a brutal assault on Englishmen visiting Fatshan was made and the now customary proceeding of capturing the Bogue forts was carried through without influencing the Governor or the populace. Ki ying was perfectly justified in considering Canton an unsafe place for Englishmen and need not be regarded as trying to overreach Sir John Davis, the new Governor of Hongkong, when he stipulated for an extension of time for two years in the matter of opening the city to foreigners. It was probably a necessary step in order to avoid further outrages on the part of the excited populace. The criticism has sometimes been made that Mr. (afterwards Sir) Rutherford Alcock handled a similar situation expeditiously enough at Shanghai, but it must be remembered that the trouble at Canton was of longer standing and went much deeper. The Governor of Canton was now the famous (or at least notorious) *Yeh Ming tsên* (of whom more anon) and under his administration things became daily more serious. Six Englishmen were murdered five months after the last outrage, while three miles from Canton, and although the offenders were promptly sought and punished by Commissioner Ki ying, there was no consequent improvement in the temper of the people. Things were in this condition when events took place, which dwarfed for the time being the anti-foreign agitation at Canton. These events are of such a magnitude that they must be treated in a separate chapter.

DEATH OF TAO KWANG. The poor Emperor had already had his sea of troubles and was now seriously ill. His fears were increased by the prediction of an eclipse of the sun for New Year's Day, 1850. This was so inauspicious an omen that the Emperor tried to avert the occurrence by postponing the New Year celebration for twenty-four hours. He might, however, as well have tried to postpone the eclipse. The sick monarch grew worse and worse, and a few weeks later died, leaving the Dragon Throne to his fourth son, Hien fêng.

NOTES

1. S. Wells Williams, "The Middle Kingdom," I, p. 400.

2. S. Wells Williams, "The Middle Kingdom," I, p. 468.

3. S. Wells Williams, "The Middle Kingdom," I, p. 409.

4. Capt. Brinkley leans sympathetically towards the Chinese side of the case while Sir Robert Douglas' view is frankly British.

5. Foster, p. 59.

6. Foster, p. 61.

7. So both Douglas and Brinkley; Pott says 20,291 chests and Dr. Arthur Brown, 22,299. The discrepancy is of no special importance.

8. "Changing China," p. 46.

CHAPTER VIII

THE TAI PING REBELLION

A D. 1850-1864.

Causes of the revolt—Hung Siu chuen—the Rebellion—religious aspect—the march on Peking—the "Ever-Victorious Army"—end of the Tai pings.

CAUSES. A pamphlet in the writer's possession contains an Episcopal charge delivered by the Rt. Rev. George Smith, first Bishop of Victoria [1] (Hongkong), in Trinity Church, Shanghai, on October 20, 1853.[2] It says on the first page: "The very walls within which we are met have been echoing the fierce sounds of battle. . . . On this very morning, yea at this very hour, within less than a mile of the edifice within which we are assembled, the booming of cannon and the noise of musketry proclaim the raging of battle and slaughter. The dead and the dying have been borne past our dwelling, the winged instruments of death have been whirled past our ears and over our heads on their message of destruction."[3] The good Bishop was well justified in adding: "China, long immovable, obeys in her turn the general law of change; dynasties and thrones are crumbling to dust." The Manchu dynasty certainly in the Tai ping rebellion had a very narrow escape, but the end was not yet.

Nevertheless, the Tai ping movement was not in its origin an antidynastic agitation. It had little in common with the secret societies which at the time were so persistent with their slogan, "Exterminate the Ts'ing; restore the Ming." With these societies the Tai pings never really co-operated. Of course there were anti-dynastic sentiments in the air which gave impetus to the rebellion. Many other elements are likewise discernible. The rottenness of the whole Imperial system, with its feet of miry clay, had been thoroughly exposed in the recent war with England. Rage at the acquisition by a foreign power of Hongkong added to the flames of discontent with the authorities at Peking. Moreover, the floods and famines from 1834 onwards, the great earthquake in Hunan in 1834, the terrible famines in Sze ch'uen from 1839 to 1841, all had their effect. Yet, notwithstanding all this, the proximate causes of the revolt were personal and religious.

Hung Siu chuen. Who was the leader in the movement which wellnigh gave to China a new religion and a new dynasty, and which actually, in the words of a Chinese annalist, "lasted fifteen years, devastated sixteen provinces, destroyed six hundred cities" and (we may add) cost the lives of at least twenty million people? It was *Hung Siu chuen*, a native of Kwangtung, a Makka by race, and a *literatus* by ambition. He made at least three attempts to pass his examinations, studied desultorily various philosophies and religions, including Christianity, but was nominally a Buddhist until the illness which marks the turning point of his career. In this illness he had a trance in which God came to him in the likeness of an old man, took out his heart and returned it to him purified, then gave him a sword and commissioned him to make war against the idolaters. On his recovery he bethought himself of the *"Good Words to Exhort the Age"* which he had received from a Christian preacher, Liang Afa, and recognized the God of his vision as the God of the Christians. Some instruction he gained from a visit to a Baptist minister, Issachar Roberts of Canton, in 1846, but Hung's Christianity was to the end of a very crude and imperfect sort, intellectually and morally. Nevertheless, he discarded idolatry, began to preach the new faith and gathered around him converts of sincerity and zeal. Together they formed the *Shang-ti hui*, or "Society of God." The leader called himself "the Younger Brother of Jesus Christ," using the term "Younger Brother" (*ti*) in its Chinese sense of subordination and obedience.

THE REBELLION. Up to 1850, as we have seen, there was little that was political in Hung's program. The conflict with the Government came through the use of the word *"hui"* ("association") which put the movement into the category of the proscribed societies. Then came the return to the old Chinese method of wearing the hair long, instead of in a queue, a custom which branded them as rebels to the Manchu authority and caused the populace to ridicule them as *Chang mao,* or *"Long-haired rebels."* But as in similar cases, the movement began with persecution to thrive and spread so rapidly in the province of Kwangsi that two Imperial Commissioners, Saishangah and Tahungah, were sent down from Peking to deal with the agitation. Then Hung took the bold step of proclaiming himself as *Tien Wang* or the "Heavenly King" and of taking for the title of the new dynasty he expected to found the name of *Tai ping* or "Perfect Peace." Never was a name more misleading adopted by a revolutionary movement! From the first Hung made for himself a trail of blood and rapine. City after city was captured and the Manchus began to fear the hour of their doom had struck. The truculent Yeh in Canton turned aside from his squabbles with the English to lament as follows: "The whole country swarms with the rebels. Our funds are nearly at an end and our troops are few; our officers disagree and the power is not concentrated. The commander of the forces wants to extinguish a burning wagon-load of faggots with a cupful of water. . . . I fear that we shall hereafter have some serious affair, that the great body of the people will rise against us and that our own followers will leave us." Yeh is said in the course of his administration to have put to death seventy thousand Taipings, yet he apparently had little or nothing to do with the suppression of the insurrection. The great soldier *Tsêng Kwo fan* did a good deal to check their advance northward, but, one after another, Yo chow, Wuchang and Kiu kiang were taken, and at last in 1853 the ancient capital, Nanking, was stormed and sacked, over twenty thousand Manchus being ruthlessly put to the sword. Here the Tien Wang now established his court, proclaimed his dynasty and appointed the Wangs of the East, North, South and West, who subsequently played an important part in the military operations. As for Hung he seems gradually to have settled down into a life of luxury and self-indulgence and to have lost the earlier enthusiasm and sincerity of his faith.

RELIGIOUS ASPECT OF THE TAI PING REVOLT. In the earliest stages of the rebellion there was much perplexity as to the proper attitude to be adopted by foreigners. The Christian complexion of the Society naturally disposed many to sympathy and even to admiration. In the charge from which I have already quoted we read: "The rebel leaders are evidently men in earnest. Their unsparing destruction of idols . . . would be impolitic in men with less lofty aims than those of a reformation of the national religion. . . . Their

compulsory prohibition of opium smoking, and
their threatened exclusion of this contraband article from the country preclude the supposition of
their being actuated by a selfish and calculating
policy." Bishop Smith goes on to describe their
camp services, Cromwellian-like preachings, to
quote from their prayers, odes and creeds. He
pictures also for us the waters of the Yang tsze
Kiang carrying down to the sea the ruins of thousands of temples and fragments of broken idols.
All this was hopeful enough. Again, from another point of view, the rebellion seemed to invite
sympathy, since there was, at least at the beginning, a desire to be on good terms with the foreigners. "Foreign nations," we read, "though far
removed, are protected and cared for by the one
great God; and China, which is so near, is under
the same gracious care. There are many men in
the world but they are all our brethren: there are
many women in the world but they are all our sisters." This also was distinctly promising, especially in view of affairs in Canton, and possibly if
strong outside influences could have secured a
footing in the counsels of the Tai ping leaders, the
insurrection might have been wisely guided to
great ends. But the fact remains that the better
acquainted foreign sympathizers became with the
Tai pings the more rapidly the sympathy melted
away. It was seen that no inroads had been
made on the polygamy of the nation and that,
if the Bible was being still studied, it was almost

exclusively in its most sanguinary and least elevated passages. So the establishment of the Tien Wang with his court at Nanking marks in a double sense the end of the first and more hopeful chapter of the story.

THE MARCH ON PEKING. The capture of Nanking seemed for a time to have exhausted the resources of the Tien Wang. Perhaps, as he had now reached the point attained by the Mings in their overthrow of the Mongol dynasty, there was felt a lack of any precedent for further movement. But new operations were manifestly necessary, and a fine, if somewhat too audacious, bid for success was made in the truly great march which was executed by General Li. It penetrated a hostile country northwards for some hundreds of miles and reached a point only a very few miles from Peking. General Li was an ex-charcoal seller, and his march in May, 1853, is described by Captain Brinkley as "one of the most extraordinary marches on record . . . like marching across one half of hostile Europe." "This intrepid commander," the historian adds, "deserves a place beside those of the great captains of the world." General Li, however, effected nothing that was permanently useful to the cause. He was checked by General Sankolinsin, and Li Hung chang, who now appears on the field of Chinese history for the first time, hung on the rebel skirts and helped to make the retreat difficult. The failure of the heroic attempt to beard the lion in his lair by carrying the rebellion to the capital of the Empire was in reality the deathblow to the Tai ping movement, though many years yet were to elapse before its final downfall. But for the energy of others than the leader it must have collapsed much earlier. Yang, who had claimed to be the Holy Spirit, and had even on one occasion exercised the privilege of scourging the Tien wang, on the strength of a revelation which had been vouchsafed him, fell into disfavor and was executed. The rebel leader remained inactive amid his thirty wives and one hundred concubines, leaving the entire management of the dubious campaign to the eleven Wangs.

"THE EVER VICTORIOUS ARMY." The real military genius whom the Tai ping revolt produced was the *Chung Wang*, whose brilliant movements against the Imperial troops on more than one occasion threatened the foreign settlements at Shanghai and elsewhere. It was this feature of the war which at length suggested the employment of foreigners to aid in putting down a rebellion as wasteful and tedious as it was bloodthirsty. The first foreigner to offer his services was Frederick Ward of Salem, Massachusetts, an adventurer under whose energetic and tactful leadership the medley hordes of recruits soon became a force to be known henceforth, and not undeservedly, under the high-sounding title, *Chang shing Kiun*, or "The Ever Victorious Army." From 1860, when this force began its career, the tide began to turn, and in 1862, when Ward was killed in action, things looked brighter for the Manchus than they had done for twelve years. Yet the "Faithful Prince" (Chang Wang) was by no means at the end of his tether, and many severe battles had yet to be fought. Ward's little army was for a time led by another American, named Burgevine, who, however, proved a failure and was dismissed by Li Hung chang, now Governor. This made way for the appointment of the young officer of engineers who was destined to be known as *"Chinese" Gordon*, until he won the yet more glorious title of "Gordon of Khartoum." The story of Charles George Gordon's wonderful influence, his knightly other-worldliness, of the splendid series of victories, of the "wand of victory" with which he led and inspired his men till they believed him invincible and invulnerable, of his chivalrous anger over Li Hung chang's breach of faith in the murder of the surrendered Wangs—all these things make up one of the most fascinating chapters in the romance of warfare. By June, 1864, Gordon's work was done; the "Ever Victorious Army" was disbanded, and the Imperial forces were left to enjoy the satisfaction of dealing the last stroke to the rebellion without foreign assistance.

THE END OF THE TAI PINGS. There was now only the capture of Nanking between the Imperialists and their goal. The Chung Wang was still a quantity to be reckoned with, but a breach was eventually made in the walls and the city was captured. The Tai ping leader poisoned himself with gold leaf and his son was captured after an heroic attempt had been made by the Chung Wang to carry him on horseback beyond the reach of the victors. Both were executed, although the execution of the "Faithful Prince" was delayed a week in order that the brave soldier might complete the writing of his memoirs. This work has been published and is an interesting record of the career of a brave and generous soldier. The victorious Imperialists sullied their triumph by digging up and desecrating the body of the Heavenly King. The whole of the fourteen years' struggle, thus brought to so tardy an end, is a long, miserable story of wasted enthusiasm and futile courage.

NOTES

1. The same year, 1844, witnessed the consecration of two Bishops of the Anglican Communion for China, viz.: Bishop Smith of Victoria (Hongkong) from England, and Bishop Boone of Shanghai from the United States.

2. "China, her Future and her Past," 1854.

3. A footnote on page 1 says, "During the delivery of the charge a ball struck the church."

CHAPTER IX

THE REIGN OF HIEN FÊNG

A. D. 1850-1860.

Hien fêng—the "Arrow"—second war with Great Britain—the Treaty of Tien tsin—destruction of the Summer Palace—the Russian advance—the Emperor's death.

HIEN FÊNG. Though the reign of Hien fêng was, throughout its ten years' duration, overshadowed by the murderous rivalry of the Tai pings, yet there was much else to make it memorable, even if it can lay no claim to distinction. The Emperor himself, who was nineteen when he came to the throne, had no share of his father's ability and vigor. His reign, so far as he personally is concerned, is a decade of imbecile and futile effort to fill depleted coffers. He desired to issue paper and iron money and seriously proposed to have "counters cut out of jade stone to take the place of bullion." He had the narrowest conceivable views of the functions of government, and the officials surrounding him at Court were as anti-foreign as ever. Ki ying, the one man at Canton who had labored for justice, and had in an earlier reign even petitioned for some measure of toleration for Christianity, was recalled and ordered to commit suicide in 1856.

THE "ARROW." What the compulsory surrender of the opium was in 1839, that the seizure of the lorcha "*Arrow*" was in 1856, the proximate and yet not the real cause of war with Great Britain. A lorcha is a vessel partly of Chinese and partly of foreign rig, and there were many of these vessels on the Chinese coast, engaged in doubtful varieties of business. Many of them were placed under the British flag at Hongkong, but unfortunately this was no reason for their not transforming themselves into freebooters as soon as they were outside Chinese waters. Consequently, the authorities at Canton had some reason for being suspicious when the "*Arrow*" sailed into the Pearl River on Oct. 8, 1856. It was boarded by Chinese in search of opium, the English flag hauled down, and fourteen sailors were carried off on suspicion of being concerned in piracy. As a matter of fact the foreign registry had expired fourteen days before,[1] but this was unknown to the Chinese. An immediate demand for redress was made by the British Consul, Harry Parkes, but the redoubtable Yeh decided to stand firm. Sir John Bowring,[2] the Governor of Hongkong, labored hard for peace, asking that Yeh should send the three nationals to the consulate and then make the request for their return on the charge of piracy. Yeh was, however, still obdurate, and, other things coming up to complicate the situation, Admiral Sir Michael Seymour on Oct. 23 took possession of the defenses of Canton. On the 25th he captured the Island and the Fort of Dutch Folly, and it was felt that now was the fitting time to insist on the promise to fulfill the treaty obligation, so long evaded, to open up Canton to foreign residence. In January, 1857, an attempt was made in Hongkong to poison all foreigners by putting arsenic in the morning's supply of bread. Fortunately, too much arsenic was employed, and the hideous plot miscarried. But the British authorities had by this time resolved to carry the matter further, and an application was made to the Governor General of India for five thousand troops.

Second War with Great Britain. In the war which now commenced the British had the co-operation of the French (their recent allies in the Crimea), who found a *casus belli* in the murder of a French priest in Kwangsi. On the British side Lord Elgin was sent out as High Commissioner and Plenipotentiary. The story of his arrival at Singapore to find an urgent message from Lord Canning, the Governor General of India, telling of the outbreak of the Sepoy Mutiny, and how, on his own responsibility, he diverted the troops intended for China to Calcutta, with momentous results for the British Empire and the world, is doubtless familiar to our readers. The delay in China was not serious. Lord Elgin reached Hongkong in July and soldiers to replace the troops sent on to India arived in September. Baron de Gros, the French Commissioner, arrived on the *"Audacieuse"* in October and soon after came the U. S. S. *"Minnesota,"* with Mr. Reed, and the Russian gunboat *"Amerika"* with Count Pontiatine. The ultimatum of the French and English was delivered to Governor Yeh on Dec. 10, and the bombardment and capture of Canton followed on the 27th. On Jan. 5, 1858, Governor Yeh was captured, not without some farcical episodes, and was sent a prisoner to Calcutta. He was followed to the ship by the jeers of his own countrymen, who, in common with the foreigner, had suffered from his truculence. In Calcutta his wonted energy altogether deserted him; he did not even care to read, explaining that "he already knew by heart all there was worth reading." He died in 1860.

THE TREATY OF TIEN TSIN. The Plenipotentiaries proceeded to Shanghai immediately after the capture of Canton, and thence journeyed to the Pei ho. The Taku forts were bombarded, following upon which a treaty was drawn up, in June, 1858, at Tien tsin, to be ratified in the following year. For the accomplishment of this end Lord Elgin's brother, Mr. (afterwards Sir) Frederick Bruce, was appointed, and the party prepared to go on to Peking. The Chinese, however, refused passage by way of Tien tsin and demanded that the embassy should proceed overland. On the attempt of the ships to pass the Taku forts they were treacherously fired upon and two English gunboats sunk. It was during this unfortunate engagement that Captain Tatnall of the American navy, while assisting the British marines into action, gave utterance to the historic saying, "Blood is thicker than water." Some time, let us hope, that saying will have an application more comprehensive still, even as wide as humanity itself. After the *contretemps* of the Taku forts there was nothing for Lord Elgin to do but to resume the offensive. A large force was collected under Sir Hope Grant and the allies, French and English, landed at Pei tang August 1, 1860. There was some difference of opinion between Sir Hope Grant and General Montauban as to the precise plan of campaign to be followed, but the Taku forts were eventually taken and the way lay open to Tien tsin. Lord Elgin now insisted that the Treaty of Tien tsin be ratified, and sent a party, including Messrs. Parkes and Loch, forward to Fung chow to prepare for a Convention. The story of the capture of the emissaries by the Chinese General Sankolinsin and of their sufferings during a ten days' imprisonment in a Chinese dungeon, is a familiar one. Only eleven survived out of the twenty-three Englishmen and thirteen Frenchmen who had been incarcerated. All the rest succumbed to the terrible tortures to which they were subjected. The kindness shown by the Chinese criminals who were Parkes' fellow-prisoners is almost the only redeeming feature of the story, apart from the courage of the captives themselves. However, the advance on Peking continued, the An ting gate surrendered, and on Oct. 24, 1860 the Treaty of 1858 was ratified by Prince Kung (representing the Emperor, who was now a fugitive at Jehol) and Lord Elgin. There were fifty-six articles altogether, providing, amongst other things, for the payment of an indemnity, the establishment of a permanent legation at Peking, the cession of Kowloon to England, the opening of Tien tsin as a treaty port, and an apology for the attack upon the fleet. The French treaty, which was signed on the following day, pushed matters further and, in providing for reparation to be made by the Chinese for the confiscation of all buildings or lands which had ever belonged to the Christians, paved the way for claims extending backwards a hundred and fifty years or more. This was an unjust and irritating measure, which complicated questions of land ownership such as had been regarded for generations as settled. A more serious, because surreptitious, matter was the insertion by the Jesuit interpreter, Père Delamarre, in the Chinese version of the treaty of two other provisions, "one securing that Christians should have a right to the free exercise of their religion all over China, and the other that French missionaries should have the right to rent land in all the provinces in the Empire and to buy and construct houses.   When this pious fraud was discovered, the French Minister thought it would do no good to denounce his interpreter, and therefore the treaty was treated by the French as binding, and never questioned by the Chinese; the other powers profited by it under the "most favored nation" clause.[3]

THE DESTRUCTION OF THE SUMMER PALACE. Lord Elgin felt that, inasmuch as the obstinacy and bad faith of the Court had been responsible for the protracted character of the war, a stern act of justice was necessary to reach the Imperial mind and heart.   Nevertheless, excuse it as we may, the destruction of the famous *Yuen-ming-yuen*, or Summer Palace, was a most regrettable act of vandalism.   It was almost the only thing in Peking which reminded men of the earliest glories of the dynasty.   Kang hsi had built his palace and there received ambassadors and legates from afar.   In the forty-eighth year of his reign he made of the palace a present to his son and heir, Yung chêng.   Kien lung in turn inherited it and joined the various buildings together under the name of Yuen ming yuen.   The Jesuit painters Castiglione and Altiret drew plans for the gardens and pavilions and the latter described it in 1743 as "a real, earthly paradise."   Now what Frenchmen had assisted to build Frenchmen assisted to destroy.   The incident was a ghastly prophecy of the inglorious aftermath of the Boxer revolt. No wonder Lord Elgin wrote: "War is a hateful business. The more one sees of it, the more one detests it."

THE RUSSIAN ADVANCE. Within a month from the signing of the treaties with England and France a treaty was signed, also at Peking, with Russia. By this treaty China ceded to the Colossus of the North all the territory north of the Amur and made possible the establishment of the great port of Vladivostock. Captain Brinkley alleges that General Ignatieff had played a skillful game of running with the hare and hunting with the hounds. "Outside Peking he gave to the British and French envoys useful information furnished by the Russian mission; inside Peking he persuaded the Chinese that his intervention alone had saved the Empire from permanent occupation by foreign troops." [4]

DEATH OF THE EMPEROR. Hien fêng had doubtless been shaken in health as well as in complacency by his hurried flight to Jehol, and it hardly needed the appearance of a comet to create alarm. Prince Kung made a diplomatic journey to Jehol to arrange matters with regard to the succession and had hardly returned before the arrival of an Edict proclaiming the Crown Prince as heir. The further news of the Emperor's death on August 22 soon reached the capital and the new Emperor was immediately proclaimed under the title of Ki tsiang.

NOTES

1.   Oliphant says "more than a month."   For all
the events described in these paragraphs see "A
Narrative of Lord Elgin's Mission," by Lawrence
Oliphant.

2.   Better known perhaps as the author of the
hymn "In the Cross of Christ I Glory," than as Governor of Hongkong.

3.   "Changing China," p. 47.

4.   Brinkley, "China," XII, p. 50.

CHAPTER X

THE REIGN OF TUNG CHIH

A. D. 1861-1875.

Prince Kung's Coup d'état—the Empress Tsz hsi—the fiasco of the fleet—Sir Robert Hart —The Burlinghame Mission—Chinese immigration—the Tien tsin massacre—the Muhamadan rebellion—trouble in Central Asia—trouble with Japan—the Emperor's marriage—Audience given to the Foreign Ministers—death of Tung chih.

PRINCE KUNG'S COUP D'ÊTAT. Prince Kung, the sixth son of Tao kwang and brother of the deceased Emperor Hien fêng, had not sized up the situation at Jehol a moment too soon. There a coterie of intriguing courtiers, prominent amongst whom were Prince I and Prince Ching, with the statesman Su Shun, had possession of the child Emperor and proposed to inaugurate their command of the situation in connection with the funeral ceremonies of Hien fêng at Peking. Prince Kung, with admirable insight into the affair, at once secured a sufficient body of troops under General Shêng Pao, produced an edict (supposedly confided to him by the late sovereign just before his death), appointing as Regents the two

PEKING (FROM AN OLD PRINT)

Empresses Dowager, namely, the widow of Hien fêng and the mother of the new Emperor. He then seized the offending princes and Su Shun. The latter was executed, the two former permitted to strangle themselves, and the *coup d'état* was accomplished. To make clear the absoluteness of their authority, Prince Kung and the two Empresses now proclaimed the four-year-old boy Emperor under the new title of *Tung chih*.

THE EMPRESS DOWAGER TSZ HSI. Of the two Empresses the legal wife of Hien fêng was *Tsz An* and generally known as the Eastern Empress. She was distinguished for her womanly virtues, but played no important personal part in the politics of her time. It was quite the reverse with her fellow Regent, the illustrious *Tsz Hsi*, who more than any ruler of China for the last hundred years deserves, for her capacity and her strength of character, the epithet of "Great." She was born in 1834 and rose from a somewhat lowly position to become the secondary wife of Hein fêng and the mother of the heir. Thence she continued to rise till "by sheer ability, by her own wits, will and shrewdness, she attained the supreme power." Of the private character of this notable personality the most diverse views have been taken and we must look to the events which she more or less controlled to do their part in interpreting that side of her career to us. In later years, after the terrible days of Boxerdom, many foreigners were enabled to get close to this wonderful woman, and it is remarkable that those who were closest and most intimate have been to a large extent the most enthusiastic as to her general womanly qualities. For example, Mrs. Conger, wife of the American Minister at the time of the Boxer troubles, sums up her estimate as follows: "Through this woman's life one catches a glimpse of the hidden quality of China's womanhood. It savors of a quality that might benefit that of the Western world. The Empress Dowager of China loved and honored her great country: that country loved and honored its great ruler. May China continue to honor her commendable deeds and make it possible for the world to place her name among the makers of history." [1] In person Tsz Hsi was tall and erect, with pronounced Tatar features, eyes piercing as those of an eagle and a voice made for the exercise of authority. But forty-seven years of more or less constant pre-occupation with the cares of state lay before the Empress in 1861, so that we must not anticipate any judgment on her career.

The Fiasco of the Fleet. It will be remembered that the Tai ping rebellion was still engaging the resources of the Empire. This circumstance, which, together with the operations of the French and English, made plain the potential usefulness of an armed flotilla, led to the suggestion from Prince Kung, seconded by the British Minister, Sir Frederick Bruce, that China should proceed to equip herself in this respect. The occupation of the native city of Shanghai by the rebels had also suggested the collection of the maritime duties by three foreign officials appointed for the purpose by England, France and the United States.   After the Treaty of Tien tsin the advantages of the plan were so obvious, through the assurance given to the Chinese Government of a reliable source of revenue, that the plan was continued, the collectorship, however, being left in the hands of England alone.   In 1862 the Inspector General of Maritime Customs was Mr. Horatio Lay, and as he happened at the time to be in London, it was to him that Prince Kung entrusted the business of buying a fleet.   Whether, as Brinkley suggests, "the magnitude of the trust disturbed Mr. Lay's mental equilibrium," or whether he really misunderstood the character of the task assigned him, the fact remains that when eight vessels arrived in China under Captain Sherard Osborn, who was given to understand that he was to receive orders only from Peking and through Mr. Lay, there was at once a considerable display of consternation.   In consequence, the fleet remained inactive and Sir Frederick Bruce was obliged to come to the rescue on behalf of the British Government.   The fleet was returned to England for sale, Mr. Lay was dismissed, and the visions of China as a great naval power faded away into thin air.   One good result followed in the appointment of Robert Hart to succeed the unfortunate Mr. Lay.

Sir Robert Hart. Foreigner as he was, no one better deserves a place in any history of China than the man who for so many years was known as "the great I. G." The honors which he was entitled to wear, and which, as he said, made him look like a Christmas Tree were not only from the rulers and learned societies of the world at large, but also from the land he loved and served so well. He had the Red Button of the first class, Ancestral Rank of the first class of the first order for three generations and the Brevet title of Junior Guardian of the Heir Apparent. Born in Ireland and graduating from college in Belfast in 1853, he went out to China in a subordinate position in H. B. Majesty's Consular service. Thence he rose until his entry upon the duties of Inspector General in the Chinese Maritime Customs brought out and developed his wonderful powers of organization. The secret of his success lay in his loyalty and in his capacity for hard work. "I long schooled myself," he wrote in 1893, "into taking an interest in my work and regarding work done as work's best reward." [1] What the work was the present condition of the Chinese Customs service is sufficient to show. Even outside of this, out of mere good-natured readiness to help out an embarrassed Government, Hart's achievements have been sufficiently notable. One illustration is afforded in the successful negotiation of the Treaty with France in 1885. Nine months passed, 80,000 taels had been expended in telegrams; then all at once came the decisive message from Sir Robert on March 31: "Signez sans delai mais ne signez pas premier avril." To write of Sir Robert's services to China adequately would be to write a book. The brave old man had his faith in China sadly shaken by the Boxer Revolt in which his house with all its priceless treasures perished, but he took his part cheerfully in the defense of the Legation and, when all was over, his volume of Essays, "These from the Land of Sinin," showed no abatement of generous judgment. He died Sep. 21, 1911, and we may fitly adopt for our own the words of an obituary notice in the London *Times* on the following day: "With his remarkable personality and wide range of sympathy, deep learning and almost poetic imagination, Sir Robert Hart endeared himself to a very wide circle of friends and acquaintances. His character was as complex as his personality was sympathetic. The Spartan training of a Belfast Irishman was tempered through his long residence in the East to a broad and tolerant acceptance of life in all its phases. Upon the traditions of a Puritan stock was grafted the easy-going philosophy of the East; and the combination of these qualities made up a character that stands out against the background of modern Chinese history as romantic a figure as that of General Gordon. . . . Taking him all in all, Sir Robert Hart leaves behind him a record as an administrator that has been rarely excelled and an example from which the Chinese in the long run cannot fail to derive guidance and benefit."

THE BURLINGHAME MISSION.[2]   A striking departure from precedent was made in 1867 in the determination of the Imperial Government to send abroad its envoys. The choice fell upon the Hon. Anson Burlinghame, who had filled for several years the post of U. S. Minister with great acceptance. With him were associated Chi Kan and Sun Kia Kü together with several secretaries and students. Their avowed object was to inform the American and European world of China's desire for progress and, so far as Mr. Burlinghame was concerned, this was done with an enthusiasm which somewhat misled some of his hearers. The foreign public became immediately attracted by the announced longing of the far East for railways, telegraphs and shipping. In consequence a serious reaction was produced as soon as it was learned that the desire of China for these things had been somewhat overstated. Nevertheless, Mr. Burlinghame's Mission was not without good results. It gave to the world a more sympathetic picture of China than it had heretofore possessed and showed that the Empire was no longer insensitive to foreign opinion. Unfortunately, Mr. Burlinghame's sudden death at St. Petersburg, February, 1870, cut short and rendered incomplete the mission he had undertaken. In the meantime he had visited the United States, England, France and Prussia.

Chinese Immigration.   One thing secured as a result of the Burlinghame Mission to the United States was the signing of a treaty in July, 1863 which is specially interesting to us to-day as encouraging the immigration of Chinese to America." The Treaty "cordially recognizes the inherent and inalienable right of man to change his home and allegiance." The first arrival of Chinese in the United States was in 1848 when two men and one woman arrived at San Francisco in the brig "*Eagle*." Then came the discovery of gold and the lure drew men from every part of the earth. In 1852 over two thousand Chinese came. At first they were cordially welcomed and, in the light of later events, it is interesting to note that at a meeting held in San Francisco, Jan. 1853, the following resolution was unanimously adopted on the motion of Mr. H. H. Haight, afterwards Governor of California: "*Resolved*, That we regard with pleasure the presence of greater numbers of these people among us *as affording the best opportunity of doing them good and through them of exerting an influence in their native land*." Later, when the number of Chinese had increased to some forty-five thousand, the opportunity of "doing them good" was forgotten and sensational fears were entertained lest the Chinese should swamp American institutions and corrupt American morals. In this way prejudice was created and fanned until Congress passed the Restriction Act of 1882 which was amended in 1884 and re-enacted in 1903.

The Massacre at Tien Tsin. It was quite natural that the French treaty of 1860, with its insistence on claims to property dating back to the 17th Century, should create a bad popular feeling, but no one could have foreseen the terrible manner in which this feeling would eventually manifest itself. As in the days of the Roman Empire, when Christians were suspected of all manner of unnatural crimes and vices, so amongst the uneducated masses of China. The stories of kidnapping and making of medicine out of children's eyes were readily believed and in some cases the belief was encouraged by those in a position to know better. Unfortunately, too, the Roman Catholic Orphanages were not always careful to explain the eagerness with which they welcomed children to their institutions. Thus when deaths occurred, as of course they would, not infrequently, there was all too much material upon which to build a terrible fabric of misunderstanding. The massacre of Tientsin, which took place in June, 1870, was the result of popular panic, induced under these circumstances, and of the excitable temperament of the French consul, M. Fontanier, who resented the appointment of a Chinese Committee of investigation. The investigation of the Orphanage in question was the very thing the French authorities should have welcomed and even courted. But M. Fontanier drove the gentlemen sent to investigate from the premises and a little later at the *yamên* of Chunghow drew his sword, struck the table, and fired two shots from his revolver at the Commissioner. Pushed to the door, he then fired into the hostile crowd outside and was thereupon murdered by the infuriated mob. The populace then attacked the Cathedral, massacred ten Sisters of Mercy, two priests, four other French subjects and three Russians. In addition to the Cathedral, which was a constant annoyance to the Chinese as standing on elevated ground, eight Protestant Churches were wrecked, after which the mob calmed down. An investigation was ordered and, after pressure had been put upon the Government by a joint note from the seven foreign ministers, punishment was meted out to certain offenders. Possibly the men punished were only what is known as "purchased criminals," but Chung how was sent to France to apologize for the outrage against French citizens. The wave of anti-foreign feeling in the meantime rose very high and the discussion of the whole problem of missionary work in China assumed grave importance.

THE MUHAMADAN REBELLION. The province of Yunnan had been largely peopled by Muhamadans, possibly since T'ang times, and recruits to the faith had constantly arrived from Koko Nor. During the Tai ping rebellion they had been grievously oppressed by the mandarins, and at length, goaded to rebellion, had taken the cities of Tali fu and Yunnan fu. The two leaders were at first Ma and Tu. The former after a while returned to Manchu allegiance and fought against his former associates. The officials seem to have had the usual idea of suppressing the rebellion by a campaign of extermination, but the Panthay leader, Tu, kept open his communications through Burmah for the supply of arms and ammunition, gained widespread acknowledgment as the Sultan Suleiman, and even sent his adopted son Hassan to obtain aid from England. Next year the Chinese forces, set free by the ending of the Tai ping rebellion, besieged Tali fu, and the city was reduced to the direst extremities. Tu endeavored to purchase safety for the people of the city by the surrender of himself, but it was his lifeless body which the Chinese general received, as Tu poisoned himself whilst being borne in his sedan chair to the appointment. His head was preserved in honey and sent to the Emperor, whilst, in defiance of the promise given, thirty thousand men, women and children perished in one indiscriminate butchery. Sultan Suleiman's death took place on Jan. 15, 1873.

Trouble in Central Asia. Quite independently, apparently, of the Panthay rebellion in Yunnan, there broke out an insurrection in the provinces of Shen si and Kan suh, which spread into Central Asia and inflamed the ever-restless ambition of the tribes of Kashgaria. A plot against the lives of two Commissioners sent to investigate was avenged by the order given for a general massacre of all followers of Islam. In some cities this was averted by the Muhamadans turning the tables on their assailants and in Khokand a surviving son of Jehangir raised the standard of rebellion, aided by a much more efficient soldier than himself, the famous Yakoob Khan. In a little while Yakoob threw off his pretense of subordination and was acknowledged by the Amir of Bokhara as Athalik Ghazi. The disturbances spreading to Ili brought the Russians upon the scene, who gave formal notice to China of their intention to occupy the country till the rebellion was subdued. Meanwhile the Imperial Government was moving, if slowly, and General *Tso Chung t'ang* with remarkable skill set about a patient and persistent reconquest of the country. His army is sometimes known as the "agricultural army" on account of the plan adopted of supplying themselves with the necessary food by lengthy sojourns at the successive oases where crops could be produced. In this way they advanced slowly but surely, across the desert, sowing and reaping. Patient tactics of this sort, reinforced by undoubted skill and valor in battle, at last broke the formidable power of Yakoob Khan. The defeated leader fled to Korla, where he died, probably from poison. The rebellious cities of Yarkand and Khotan submitted and peace was restored in 1878.

TROUBLE WITH JAPAN. In entirely another direction China had found herself within measurable distance of another war which might not have ended so fortunately. The island of Tai wan, or Formosa, had always been a very troublesome appanage to China, and the Government seldom concerned itself with the district as long as there was no open rebellion. In 1868, however, Japan had occasion to protest against the massacre of over fifty sailors from the Riu Kiu Islands. The Imperial Government maintained at first that the murdered islanders were China's own subjects, but the Japanese pushed matters to the extent of landing a punitive force, and the Chinese ultimately consented, through the good offices of Sir Thomas Wade, to pay the expenses of the expedition, while the claim of the Japanese to the Riu Kiu Islands was tacitly acknowledged.

The Marriage of Tung chih. By 1872 the young Emperor had reached the age of sixteen, and it was determined to provide him with a consort. The Empress Dowager chose for this high honor the lady *Ahluta*, daughter of a distinguished *literatus*, and the wedding was celebrated with great ceremony on Oct. 16, 1872. As the marriage of an Emperor was always assumed to mark his coming of age, the Empresses took the opportunity to surrender into the hands of Tung chih the responsibilities of government on Feb. 23, 1873.

Audience Given to Foreign Ministers. Following upon the marriage of the Emperor an event took place of the greatest possible significance. On June 15, 1873, the following Edict appeared: "The Tsung li Yamên having presented a memorial to the effect that the Foreign Ministers residing in Peking have implored us to grant an audience that they may deliver letters from their governments, we command that the Foreign Ministers residing in Peking, who have brought letters from their Governments, be accorded audience. Respect this." The audience was given in the "Pavilion of the Purple Light," where it had been usual to receive the tribute-bearing envoys from the barbarians. Six ministers attended, representing Japan, England, the United States, France, Russia and Holland. This was on the 29th of June, 1873. The representatives of the powers were not received in the precincts of the palace proper until 1894.

Death of Tung chih. The Empresses had not long to regret their freedom from the cares of state. At the beginning of January, 1875, the youthful Emperor was reported as "happily" suffering from smallpox and on the 12th of the month he passed over to the ancestors. Whether his death was superinduced by poison will never be known. Suspicion is aroused by the fact that the young Empress Ahluta, together with her unborn babe, died two months afterwards. The two Dowagers at once proclaimed the four-year-old child of Prince Chun, the seventh son of Hien fêng. Thus the succession passed for the first time out of the direct line of the Manchu dynasty.

NOTES

1. *"Letters from China,"* p. 377. See also *"Court Life in China,"* by Dr. Isaac T. Headland; *"China's New Day,"* by the same author.

2. An account of the life and mission of Anson Burlinghame has just been published by Mr. Frederick Wells Williams.

CHAPTER XI

THE REIGN OF KWANG HSU

A. D. 1875-1898.

Accession of Kwang hsu—the Margary affair —China's first railway—the restoration of Kuldja—trouble over Korea—war with France —marriage of the Emperor—anti-Christian riots —war with Japan—the treaty of Shimoneseki— European aggressions—the Reform movement— Chang Chih tung—Kang Yu wei—the Reform Edicts of Kwang hsu—the Empress' coup d' etat.

ACCESSION OF KWANG HSU. The child Tsai t'ien had been posthumously adopted as the son of Tung chih and was now placed upon the throne under the name of *Kwang hsu,* "Illustrious Succession." The placing of another child upon the Dragon Throne enabled the masterful Dowager, mother of the late Emperor, to exercise an almost undisputed power for the greater part of the new reign. Those who gained access to the Emperor from the outer world have reported favorably of his intellectual capacity and character, and there can be little doubt as to his genuine desire for reform. But probably he combined with his good intentions some lack of judgment and a by no means unexplainable inexperience of affairs. It is in any case evident that his personality had in it nothing which could make headway against the masterfulness of his aunt, who certainly in these years deserved the description so often applied to her, of "the only man in China."

THE MARGARY AFFAIR. Partly arising out of the Muhamadan rebellion in Yunnan, which had maintained communications with Burmah for the sake of getting weapons and supplies, and following the signing of the treaty of 1862 between Great Britain and Burmah, the desire had been growing in India for new trade connections with China through the south-western provinces. Hence a mission had been arranged for and passports issued by the Government at Peking to a party under Col. Browne. To this party Mr. Augustus Margary, a member of the Chinese consular service, had been attached. He set out to meet the rest of the expedition at Bhamo and accomplished his mission in safety. Then on the return journey he was attacked by Chinese troops at the small town of Manwyne and treacherously murdered. This happened in February, 1875. Col. Browne with great difficulty, and largely through the bravery of the Sikh troops who accompanied him, made his way back to Bhamo. The outrage led to prolonged investigations and negotiations, carried on mainly by Sir Thomas

Wade and Li Hung chang. These resulted finally in the *Chi fu Convention* of Sept. 13, 1876. By this Convention China agreed to send a mission of apology to England, to proclaim throughout the Empire the right of foreigners to travel, and to pay an indemnity of 200,000 taels. Several ports of call on the Yang tsz river were also opened for trade and one further result was the establishment of a permanent representative of China at the English Court.

China's First Railway. Perhaps we should say, "the first steam railway," for, according to the Vicomte D'Ollone, "the Chinese invented the railway," and he describes how, on the borders of Tibet, "in the flagstones which form the pavement two little channels are cut, which all wheelbarrows follow, coming or going." [1] It was more difficult to recommend to China the railway of the Westerner and the "iron horse," but this is how the first experiment came about. In the first years of Kwang hsu terrible famines had visited China. It is estimated that nine million people perished in the four provinces of Chih li, Shan si, Ho nan and Kan suh alone. A very active part in the relief measures was taken by Li Hung chang, who for the first time was led to experience the inefficiency of Chinese methods of transportation. Under these circumstances a company of foreign merchants undertook to construct a railway from Shanghai to Wu sung, a distance of twelve miles. The innovation aroused all the prejudices of Chinese conservatism. The populace feared for the graves of the ancestors, the boatmen were troubled about the imminent competition, the believers in *fêng shui*[2] trembled lest the luck of the land should be disturbed, and most men disliked the probable extension of foreign influence. Hence, no sooner was the line in operation, than the Chinese determined to make it permanently inoperative. They walked deliberately in front of the engine, to transform themselves from hostile but comparatively ineffective human beings into even more hostile and terribly potent spirits. The excitement increased to such an extent that the Government was constrained to buy up the line, tear up the rails and dump the engines into the river. The rails were, eventually, we believe, exported to Formosa, but no more attempts were made to build railways in China till 1881, when Wu Ting fang had influence enough to secure the construction of the line to the capital.

THE RESTORATION OF KULDJA. We have already followed to its close the suppression of Yakoob Khan's rebellion in Kashgaria, but it will be remembered that Russia had taken advantage of the uncertain situation in order to occupy Kuldja. After the fall of Kashgar, Dec. 17, 1877, demands were made on Russia for the return of the occupied territory. To effect this, Chung how, whom we have already encountered as heading the mission of apology to France after the Tien tsin massacre, was sent to St. Petersburg. The wily Muscovite so far overreached the Chinese diplomat that the latter returned with the *Treaty of Livadia,* by means of which the return of Kuldja was promised on the payment of five million rubles. This to China seemed like paying too high a price for the return of her own property, and a storm of indignation broke upon the head of the ambassador. Prince Ch'un, the Emperor's father, clamored for war, and the future Viceroy Chang Chih tung appears upon the scene clamorous for Chung how's head. The unfortunate diplomat was sentenced to decapitation, a sentence which would undoubtedly have been carried out but for a personal letter from Queen Victoria. The respited official retired into private life and died, less summarily, of creeping paralysis in 1893. A new instrument for diplomacy appeared in the famous *Marquis Tsêng,* son of the General Tsêng Kwo fan, who had rendered noteworthy service against the Tai pings. Tsêng, who had taught himself English with the help of Murray's Grammar and a Nuttall's Dictionary, had become Minister to Great Britain, and he was now sent to St. Petersburg to obtain something more satisfactory than the Treaty of Livadia. He succeeded admirably and the new treaty was ratified Aug. 19, 1881. We may add here that the Marquis Tsêng subsequently, in 1885, arranged the Opium Convention with Great Britain, was a member of the

Tsungli Yamên, served on the Admiralty Board and the Board of Revenue and died, full of honors, in 1890. Among other faculties possessed by him in addition to those of the diplomat, we may mention his calligraphy. Even the Emperor was glad to obtain specimens of his skill in this department of art and literature combined.

Trouble over Korea. Affairs had not been straightened out in Kashgaria before they began to assume a gloomy complexion in Korea. The peninsula had been long regarded as a tributary nation but, as in Formosa, little trouble was taken with the government so long as Korea did not embroil China with other powers. Unfortunately this was just what happened not infrequently. The persecution of Christianity in Korea involved the murder of some French missionaries in 1866; an American ship was burned and its crew murdered; and Japan had commercial grievances of long standing. As China seemed very anxious to disclaim responsibility the Japanese cleverly took advantage of the situation and concluded a treaty directly with Korea in which the independence of the principality was assumed. China, thus outwitted, endeavored to regain lost ground by means of intrigue and factions arose leading to so unsatisfactory a condition that the two countries were brought more than once to the very verge of war. Ultimately, following upon several tragic episodes, a *modus vivendi* was found by Li Hung chang and Count Ito, by which the troops of the nations were withdrawn. This agreement kept the peace until 1894. It was further agreed that, in case either nation felt it necessary to send troops into Korea, due notice of the intention should be given.[3]

WAR WITH FRANCE. Some territory had been obtained from China by France as far back as 1787. In 1858 a further advance had been made by the taking of Saigon and the consequent extension of French influence through Cochin China and Cambodia. For this treaty recognition was obtained in 1862. After the Franco-German war France began to seek a restoration of prestige in her Colonial Empire. A treaty was made with Annam in 1874 without consultation with the suzerain power, by which the Red River and its ports, Hai phong and Hanoi, were opened for trade. Since this territory was used for the opening up of trade routes into Yun nan the French soon found themselves in difficulties with the guerilla troops known as Black Flags (largely made up of fugitives from the insurrectionary wars in Yun nan), with the secret support, it was believed, of the Chinese Government behind them. No war was declared on either side, but the French, in carrying on her "reprisals," soon came face to face with the regular Chinese troops and warlike operations continued during 1883 and 1884. A convention drawn up at Tien tsin by Li Hung chang and Captain Fournier would have put an end to the conflict, but for the impatience of the French in taking possession of the awarded territory before the Chinese general had received orders from his superior. The consequence was a conflict in which the French were worsted and the "reprisals" continued, without any declaration of war. Among the incidents were the unjustifiable attack by Admiral Courbet upon the forts and ships at Fu chow and the bombardment of Ke lung. It was to the relief of all parties, the French included, that, through the good offices of Sir Robert Hart, a treaty was at last signed in June, 1885, by which much the same terms were accepted as had been agreed upon by Li Hung chang a year earlier. Tong king now became French, but China came out of the struggle, from a military point of view, not discreditably. It was at this time that Li Hung chang's plans for a new navy began to take shape under Admiral Lang and that a new Navy Department was created under Prince Chun, the Emperor's father. The exigencies of the war with France also led to the extension of telegraph lines which, strangely enough, did not arouse the superstitious prejudice of the people as had been the case with the railways.

MARRIAGE OF THE EMPEROR. In March, 1889, the marriage of the young Emperor took place with unusual splendor. The lady honored by the Imperial choice (*i. e.* not of Kwang hsu, but of the Empress dowager) was Yehonala, a niece of Tsze hsi. The festivities were on an extraordinary scale, and a large number of honors were distributed to signalize the occasion. The event marked also the assumption of sovereignty by the Emperor and the end of Tsz hsi's second regency. An Edict issued at the time announces: "The Emperor is now advancing to manhood, and the greatest respect which he can pay to us will be to discipline his own body, to develop his mind, to pay unremitting attention to the administration of the Government, and to love his people." Two years later Kwanghsu gave his first audience to the foreign ministers, held, as the audience of the reign of Tung chih had been, in the Hall of the Tribute-bearers. It was given out as the Emperor's intention to hold these audiences annually in the first month.

ANTI-CHRISTIAN RIOTS. The year 1891 was rendered notorious for the anti-foreign and anti-Christian riots in Hu nan and the Yang tsze kiang valley. The vilest calumnies had been spread broadcast against the Christians, notably by one Chow Han, a scholar of sufficient culture to know better. Puns on such words as *Tien Chu* (Lord of Heaven) and *Yang jên* (foreign men) enabled the caricaturists to depict the God of the Christians as the "Heavenly Pig" and the white men as the "Goat men." The Tsung li Yamên was powerless to check the riots and the payment of money indemnities but poorly atoned for the cruel murder of missionaries and their converts. One good result, however, was the issuance of an

Imperial Edict to this effect: "The propagation of Christianity by foreigners is provided for by treaty, and Imperial decrees have been issued to the provincial authorities to protect the missionaries from time to time. . . . The doctrine of Christianity has for its purpose the teaching of men to be good."

WAR WITH JAPAN. Some years before, Li Hung chang had written the words: "It is above all things necessary to strengthen our country's defenses, to organize a powerful navy, and not to undertake aggressive steps against Japan in too great a hurry." Unfortunately for China the recommendations of the great statesman were only half followed. The division of the fleet into Northern and Southern without mutual responsibility proved to be disastrous and in 1894 all the prestige gained by China in the contest with France was dissipated like a morning mist. Into the causes of this memorable war it is impossible here to go in detail. They have been summarized somewhat as follows: 1. The rankling sense of injustice created in 1884; 2. The assassination of the Korean statesman, Kim Ok kuin, who had been decoyed from Japan by Korean emissaries and murdered in Shanghai; 3. The feeling that, as Japan had opened Korea to the world, her influence should be something more than nominal; 4. The unrest in Japan, which made foreign war an easy way out of a difficult domestic situation. The actual determining cause for the unsheathing of the sword was the sending of Chinese troops into Korea without prompt notice given to Japan.

THE CAMPAIGN. Hostilities actually began with the sinking of the English steamer *Kowshing*, which was being used as a transport for the Chinese troops, on July 25, 1894. War was declared August 1 and troops were hurried to the Yalu. The battle of Pingyang was fought September 15, six thousand Chinese being slain and the remainder fleeing northward in a most demoralized condition. It was in this battle that the Chinese general, who had ascended a hill to direct the fight with his fan, learned, and the Chinese government through him, that the old order in the Orient was doomed. Two days later the naval battle of the Yalu was fought on somewhat more equal terms. The Chinese made a good fight, but lost four ships. The actual invasion of China commenced October 24, with the Japanese forces under Count Oyama. The advance was marked by great military skill and the desire to gain, so far as possible, the good will of the populace by whom they passed. The famous fortress of Port Arthur was stormed on November 21, with a loss of only four hundred men, a victory which was marred by a cruel massacre such as sadly tarnished the luster of the Japanese arms. In the advance into Manchuria the Japanese forces had been equally successful, and it was becoming plain that it might be well to consider terms of peace.

Mr. Detring was sent to Japan on November 27 to open up negotiations, but he had no proper credentials and was not received. Before a second attempt could be made the capture of Hai cheng and Kai ping made the Japanese masters of the whole of the Liao tung peninsula. Two Chinese emissaries had meanwhile been sent to treat for peace, but they too were insufficiently accredited. The great battle of Wei hai wei followed in February, 1895, and by land and by sea the Japanese forces were completely victorious. The one Chinese hero of the war, Admiral Ting, after hoisting his flag of surrender, committed suicide in his cabin. The Southern fleet, which all the while was anchored in the Yang tsz kiang, according to the theory that the war concerned the North exclusively, might have turned the scale of the war had it chosen to intervene. The capture of Yin kow in Manchuria now brought the hitherto despised "dwarf men" so near the gates of Peking that a serious effort for peace had become imperative.

THE TREATY OF SHIMONESEKI. The emissary this time was no other than Li Hung chang himself. He left for Japan on March 15 and soon after arrival was shot at by an over-zealous Japanese patriot. The shot, which fortunately was not fatal, cost Japan a good deal, since it led to the granting of an armistice of some weeks (except in the case of the campaign in Formosa), and undoubtedly helped to secure for China more favorable terms than she could otherwise have expected. A treaty was drawn up and signed at Shimoneseki on April 17. It was ratified at Chifu on May 8 and provided for the independence of Korea, the cession of the Liao-tung peninsula, Formosa and the Pescadores, the payment of two hundred million taels indemnity, and the opening of certain ports in Hu peh, Szechu'en, Kiang su and Cheh Kiang. Afterwards, on pretense of maintaining the integrity of China, the three powers of Russia, Germany and France stepped in to rob Japan of the fruits of her victory, so far as the Continental acquisitions were concerned. The Liao tung peninsula was given up and a further indemnity of thirty million taels accepted instead. So came to its close a campaign in which China's reputation for military and naval strength collapsed like a pricked balloon.

EUROPEAN AGGRESSION. The sixtieth birthday of the Empress Dowager, which under ordinary circumstances would have been celebrated with lavish splendor, and for which great preparations had been made, came at a dark hour in Chinese history, but we may regard as an omen of good for the future that among the presents received was a New Testament in a silver casket, which was presented by the English and American ambassadors and graciously received. For the present, however, the Empress had but little reason for looking kindly upon the ways of the foreigners. The collapse of China before the new might of Japan had aroused the greed of the nations who regarded "the slicing of the melon" as an inevitable operation in which he who came earliest was likely to get most.   Hence the conclusion of peace with Japan inaugurated a period of aggression which led in time to dire results. Russia having posed as China's friend in the saving of the Liao tung peninsula and in the provision by loan of the means for paying the indemnity, felt entitled to repay herself, by means of the so-called Cassini Convention, in the leasing of Port Arthur, March, 1898.   Germany had already taken her reward in the seizure of the Bay of Kia chao in Shan tung, November, 1897. The reason given was the murder of two German missionaries who had been slain as a matter of fact to get the local magistrate into trouble. Great Britain countered the Russian move by obtaining a lease of Wei hai wei [4] on April 2, 1898, and France, on May 2, obtained Kwang chou wan.   "By 1899," writes Mr. A. J. Brown,[5] "in all China's three thousand miles of coast line, there was not a harbor in which she could mobilize her own ships without the consent of the hated foreigner."   Yet Italy had the assurance to demand the Bay of Sam mên in Cheh kiang and might have obtained it had not the power by this time passed once more into the vigorous hands of the great Empress Dowager.

THE REFORM MOVEMENT.   The agitations in the Empire had hitherto been largely in the hands of the secret societies and had had for their object little beyond the vague program, "Destroy the Ts'ing; restore the Ming." From this time onwards a new spirit was abroad in the land. It was the result of many co-operating causes. The success of Japan had been clearly due to the fact that the Island Empire had adopted Occidental methods. The infiltration of Western learning, through the labors of missionaries and others, was beginning to tell. Most effective of all, there were personalities at work with a very definite end in view.

CHANG CHIH TUNG. One of the most influential of these was the great viceroy of Hu peh, Chang Chih tung, whose book, known by its English title, *"China's Only Hope,"* [6] is said by a competent authority to have "made more history in a shorter time than any other modern piece of literature." Advertised throughout China on yellow posters, introduced with a rescript from the Emperor himself, it "astonished a kingdom, convulsed an empire and brought on a war." It was by no means the work of a radical. Chang Chih tung was no advocate of Parliaments. "There were too many fools," he said naively. Nor was he too favorable to the introduction of foreign instructors. They seemed to him too lazy, and inclined to dribble out their knowledge to students in order to make their engagement last longer. But he was in some respects thoroughgoing. With regard to opium he said:

"Cast out the poison." With regard to education: "Abolish the eight-legged essay," whilst he recommended that the temples of the two religions in which he did not believe should be turned into schools. Above all he urged loyalty to the throne, to the race and to Confucianism. The book won authority from the man himself. Born in 1835, scholar, governor, viceroy, founder of universities and iron works, promoter of coal mining and cotton spinning, a brilliant statesman and an ardent patriot, Chang Chih tung certainly deserved well of his countrymen. He died in 1910 respected by foreigners for his straightforward honesty and having accomplished a great deal towards guiding the feet of young China into the path of safe and sane reform.[7]

KANG YU WEI. A character harder to estimate aright is that of "China's modern sage," Kang Yu wei,[8] a Cantonese, whose studies on the restoration in Japan, the decadence of Turkey, the constitutional changes in England, and the life of Peter the Great, penetrated in 1897 into the royal palace. Kang Yu wei's friends have declared he was by no means so precipitate as the Emperor's later actions would imply and his friendship with Chang Chih tung would argue for a certain measure of conservatism. His influence, however, is unmistakable. As Secretary of the Tsungli Yamên and as publisher of a periodical entitled *News for the Times* he had ample opportunity to reach and influence others.

Almost before the argus-eyed Dowager was aware
of what was going on in the palace precincts the
Emperor was surrounded by persons and influences recommended by Kang Yu wei. For three
months "the modern Confucius" reigned supreme
in the Emperor's counsels; then came the deluge.

Kwang hsu's Reforms. The result of such
influences as have been described, aided by the
natural intelligence of the Emperor and his interest in western toys and scientific experiments, was
soon apparent in his acts. "We do not lack," he
said, "either men of intellect or brilliant talents,
capable of learning and doing anything they
please; but their movements have hitherto been
hampered by old prejudices." Kwang hsu was
at least resolved that this should no longer be true
of himself. In the early part of 1898 he is said
to have bought a hundred and twenty-nine foreign
books, a Bible, maps, globes and charts. Moreover, he was determined to make things move outside the palace and there is something pathetic in
the eagerness with which he launched, one after
another, those twenty-seven ill-fated Edicts of
July, 1898. They provided, with bewildering
haste, and with little or no attention to the means
for carrying them into execution, for every reform which his somewhat visionary instructors had
suggested to his enthusiasm. There was to be a
new university at Peking, universal reform in
education, extension of railways, developments of
art, science and agriculture, together with the im-

mediate abolition of all that had hitherto retarded the advance of the Empire. It was a beautiful dream, but the dreamer was destined to a very sudden and rude awakening.

THE EMPRESS' COUP D'ÉTAT. The Empress Dowager was, as we have seen, no novice at a coup d'état. It had become manifestly a case for instant action if she were to save herself and her friends from the consequences of the new movement. We may also give her credit for the sincere belief that the new craze for western materialism was likely to play into the hands of the greedy European powers ever on the alert for the partitioning of China. It is no reflection on her patriotism that she believed drastic measures were necessary for the Empire's salvation. Yuan Shih kai has been blamed by some for warning the Empress of what was taking place in the Royal Palace. He too may be credited with the belief that hot-headed, inexperienced young enthusiasts were not the real leaders the time necessitated. So the blow fell; Kang Yu wei escaped with difficulty to live henceforth with a price upon his head. Most of his associates were ruthlessly beheaded; the poor young Emperor was from this time forth practically deposed and a prisoner; and a new era was inaugurated by an Edict which commences as follows:

"Her Imperial Majesty the Empress Dowager, Tsz hsi, since the first years of the reign of the late Emperor Tung Chih down to our present reign, has twice ably filled the regency of the Empire, and never did her Majesty fail in happily bringing to a successful issue even the most difficult problems of government. In all things we have ever placed the interests of our Empire before those of others and looking back at her Majesty's successful handiwork, we are now led to beseech, for a third time, for the assistance from her Imperial Majesty, so that we may benefit from her wise and kindly advice in all matters of State. Having now obtained her Majesty's gracious consent, we truly consider this to be a great boon both to ourselves as well as to the people of our Empire."[9]

NOTES

1. *"In Forbidden China,"* by the Vicomte D'Ollone, p. 202.

2. Literally "Wind-water" (superstition); the geomantic philosophy of China.

3. See the *"Story of Korea"* by Joseph H. Longford, 1911; also the works of Ross, Mackenzie and Gale.

4. For an exhaustive account of Wei hai wei, read R. F. Johnston's *"Lion and Dragon in Northern China."*

5. *"New Forces in Old China."*

6. The Chinese title is *"Chüan Hsüeh Pien"* which in the French translation is "Exhortation à l'Etude" or "Exhortation to Reform." "China's only hope," is the title in Dr. S. I. Woodbridge's translation.

7. For a good account of Chang Chih tung see Dr. W. E. Geil's *"Eighteen Capitals of China,"* p 256 ff.

8. An appreciation of Kang Yu Wei as a philosopher appears in the *Hibbert Journal,* 1908.

9. The story of these days is well given by Dr. Headland in *"Court Life in China,"* and in Dr. Brown's *"New Forces in Old China."*

CHAPTER XII

THE EMPRESS DOWAGER'S THIRD REGENCY

A. D. 1898—1908.

The Edicts of September—the Empress and the Boxers—massacre of the missionaries—the Siege of the Legation—the relief of Peking—defence of the French Cathedral—the looting of Peking—the Peace negotiations—massacre at Blagovestchensk—events in Manchuria—Li Hung chang—foreign affairs—results of the Russo-Japanese war—the awakening of China—reforms of Tsz hsi—deaths of Emperor and Empress Dowager.

THE EDICTS OF SEPTEMBER. The *coup d'etat* of the Empress was successfully carried out September 22, 1898. Troops had been silently collected; the Emperor was seized and consigned to the seclusion he had doubtless intended for his aunt. Two days later the Edicts of July were all annulled. At one fell swoop the cardhouse of reform was shattered and its authors seized or scattered. The Empress astutely managed to explain and consolidate her assumption of power by holding a reception for the wives of the Ambassadors who had no alternative but to accept the situation. A year later when it was announced that the Emperor had abdicated in favor of Pu Chü, the son of Prince Tuan, the Chinese and foreign ministers were indeed genuinely concerned and put sufficient pressure on Tsz hsi to cancel the Edict of abdication. The British ambassador, moreover, hinted that the health of the incarcerated Emperor must be carefully considered or there might be consequences. So, although Kwang hsu remained in prison, there was no further talk of abdication.

THE EMPRESS AND THE BOXERS. The activity of the Dowager was not solely in the interest of her retention of power. She was seriously alarmed at the aggressions of the foreigners and had a definite policy looking towards their expulsion. In the energetic words of one of her edicts: "The various Powers cast upon us looks of tiger-like voracity, hustling each other in their endeavors to be first to seize upon our innermost territories. They think that China, having neither money nor troops, would never venture to go to war with them. They fail to understand, however, that there are certain things which this Empire can never consent to, and that, if hard pressed, we have no alternative but to rely upon the justice of our cause, the knowledge of which in our breasts strengthens our resolves and steels us to present an united front against our aggressors."

A weapon was unhappily ready to hand.   Among the anti-Manchu societies which were flourishing at the time was that known as the *I Ho kwan*, or Righteous Harmony Fist's Association, popularly known as the Boxers.   The Empress adroitly led them to reconsider their anti-dynastic prejudices and to enlist themselves in her anti-foreign campaign.   This they did with a fanatical enthusiasm which boded ill.   The Boxers were not only madly hostile to the foreigner but were profoundly convinced of their own invulnerability to the arms of the alien, and their numbers, swollen by all the elements which made for mischief, grew daily more formidable.   An alliance of anti-reformers seemed to Tsz hsi to ensure doubly the success of her plans.

MASSACRE OF THE MISSIONARIES.   The first fury of the Boxers fell upon the missionaries,[1] who were for the most part in the remoter districts of the inflamed provinces and who were, for various reasons, specially obnoxious to the mob.   Mr. Brooks, a missionary of the Church of England in Shan tung, was murdered late in 1899, and, after four months of unrest and futile negotiation, the massacres were resumed on an unprecedented scale.   Messrs. Norman and Robinson, English missionaries, were murdered in June, 1900, the mission stations of Pao ting fu were burned and their inmates slaughtered.   Dr. A. H. Smith sums up the casualties, so far as they apply to the foreign missionaries, as follows: "The devastating

Boxer cyclone cost the lives of a hundred and thirty-five adult Protestant missionaries and fifty-three children and of thirty-five Roman Catholic fathers and nine Sisters. The Protestants were in connection with ten different missions, one being unconnected. They were murdered in four provinces and in Mongolia, and belonged to Great Britain, the United States, and Sweden." We must add to these figures several thousand native converts who met their fate with unflinching heroism. But for the strong stand taken by some of the Viceroys, notably by Chang Chih tung, Yuan Shih kai, Liu Kun yi, Tuan Fang and Li Hung chang, the bloodshed would doubtless have been a thousandfold worse. Happily there were men in China at this crisis who were prepared to take the consequences of disobeying the Dowager.

THE SIEGE OF THE LEGATIONS.[2] The advance of the Boxers upon Peking soon cut off the communications of the foreign ministers with the outside world. But for the timely arrival of some four hundred and fifty marines from the warships it would scarcely have been possible to defend the Legations against the attacks which in a few days commenced. The foreign powers were beginning to realize the critical nature of the situation and poured troops into Tien tsin, but the force of two thousand men sent to relieve their fellow-countrymen in Peking proved insufficient and was forced to retire with heavy loss. Consequently the legations were "straitly shut up" within the walls of the British Embassy and disaster on a large scale seemed imminent. The chancellor of the Japanese legation, Mr. Sugiyama, was murdered on June 11 and Baron von Ketteler, the German minister, on June 20. The attack, which at times was made with the greatest possible fury, at other times appeared to be half-hearted, and it was apparent that there were divided counsels in the Chinese Court. Later investigation brought out the fact that the reactionary leader, Prince Tuan, was the most inveterate enemy of the besieged, whilst it was to Prince Jung lu that they owed their eventual escape. When the longed-for and long-expected relief came ammunition and food were well-nigh exhausted and out of the defending force of less than five hundred, sixty-five had been killed and a hundred and thirty-one wounded. Moreover, the anxiety and suffering of those within were matched by the suspense of the whole civilized world outside, ignorant and apprehensive of the fate of the besieged.

RELIEF OF THE LEGATIONS. Meanwhile a strong relief force was gathering, and on August 4 an army of twenty thousand men, Japanese, American, French, Russian, German and British, was able to start for Peking. Opposition was met at various points, but in ten days the force was within striking distance, and on August 14 General Gaselee and a party of Sikhs were the first to fight their way to the beleaguered garrison. Mrs. Conger writes: "Rejoice! All nations rejoice and give thanks. Our coming troops are outside the city wall." Simultaneously with the entry of the Allies, the Empress Dowager, the Emperor and a few attendants left hurriedly for the old capital of China, Si ngan fu.[3]

DEFENSE OF THE FRENCH CATHEDRAL. One of the most heroic episodes of the siege was the defense of the French Cathedral by Bishop Favier. He had with him eighty Europeans and three thousand four hundred native Christians, of whom two thousand seven hundred were women and children. Four hundred died during the siege, mostly buried under the ruins caused by exploding mines. Few things in the history of this terrible time are more touching than the story told by a Portuguese Sister to Mrs. Little of how the Sisters used to make the children under their care follow them in a long train to this side or that side, wherever the fire seemed the slackest, until at last one day a large number were blown up by a mine and killed.

THE LOOTING OF PEKING. An unhappy incident of the relief of the Legations was the wanton and savage destruction with which the foreign troops avenged the savagery of their foes. It is useless now to bandy reproaches among the various nationalities concerned, but it may be said that order was first restored among the Japanese, then among Americans and British. Many Chinese, perfectly innocent of complicity with Boxerdom, had occasion to rue the entrance of the foreign forces into Peking and the object lesson which it was designed to give was to a large extent spoiled. Captain Brinkley writes: "It sends a thrill of horror through every white man's bosom to learn that forty missionary women and twenty-five little children were butchered by the Boxers. But in Tung chow alone, a city where the Chinese made no resistance and where there was no fighting, five hundred and seventy-three Chinese women of the upper classes committed suicide rather than survive the indignities they had suffered." After this the looting of the treasures of *Yamêns* and private houses and the carrying off by the Germans of the beautiful astronomical instruments given by Louis XIV to Kang hsi seem insignificant. Our civilization of which we boast so much is still something of a veneer.

PEACE NEGOTIATIONS. Field Marshal General von Waldersee arrived with a German force in September, 1900, and, taking supreme command, at once started upon the complicated task of obtaining reparation for the mischief wrought. The Concert of Powers was as usual somewhat difficult to keep in tune and Russia's withdrawal for her own ends, while maintaining her claim for a very heavy indemnity, was annoying and mischievous. Ultimately the punishments were agreed upon. Certain guilty officials, eleven in number, were to receive the reward of their misdeeds, the importation of arms was forbidden for a term of years, the customary examinations were to be suspended for five years, and an indemnity of 450,000,000 taels, divided among the powers, was ordered paid. Of this last a number of the missions concerned refused to accept their share, feeling that the blood spilled was not to be valued in coin, and the United States generously arranged for its share to go to the education of the youth of China. There was further exacted a mission of apology to Germany and Japan, and memorials of the murdered Chancellor and Ambassador were to be erected in Peking, where they are currently said to be regarded as monuments in honor of the assassins.

THE MASSACRE OF BLAGOVESTCHENSK. It has already been noted that Russia had detached herself from the powers to pursue her own policy, and this involved the occupation of Manchuria, avowedly because of the disturbed condition of the country. It was the beginning of a movement not finally checked until the Japanese undertook to check it with the sword. A foul blot upon the first stage of the occupation was the terrible massacre of Chinese at Blagovestchensk on the Amur, in reprisal for an attack made by the Chinese on some Cossack troops. Thousands of men, women and children were ruthlessly driven at the bayonet point into the river. It was a crime which fitly deserved the Nemesis which was so soon to overtake the great northern power.

SUBSEQUENT EVENTS. Russia's hold on Manchuria was being tightened through the support of Li Hung chang, while Liu Kun yi and Chang Chih tung, supported by Great Britain and Japan, made so vigorous a protest that the Convention proposed by Russia was withdrawn. On September 7, 1901, the Peace Protocol was finally signed and in the same month the foreign troops, with the exception of the legation guards, were withdrawn from Peking. In October the Imperial Court returned from Si ngan fu, and on November 7 the illustrious statesman, Li Hung chang, died.

Li Hung Chang. This distinguished man was born in 1822 in the province of An hwui, graduated *chin shih* in 1847, and entered the Han lin college. He came into public notice in 1853 by raising a body of militia to operate against the Tai pings, was appointed for his services Governor of Kiang su in 1862 and at the conclusion of the rebellion in 1864 was raised to the dignity of an Earl. In 1867 he became Viceroy of Hu Kwang, and in 1870, after the Tien tsin massacre, Governor of the metropolitan province of Chih li. During the last days of Tung chih's illness Li cooperated with the Empresses Dowager for the elevation of Kwang hsu to the throne. He made with his men a forced march of eighty miles in thirty-six hours and arrived at Peking in time to get command of the situation. "Every man," says Dr. Giles, "held a wooden bit in his mouth to prevent talking, and the metal trappings of the horses were muffled." In 1876 Li Hung chang became, as we have seen, the special Commissioner to settle the Margary affair, and in this capacity drew up the Chi fu treaty. After taking a leading part in the negotiations with France in 1884, some uneventful years passed, and in 1892 he celebrated his seventieth birthday. Two years later he was drawn out of his retirement by the war with Japan and, after losing his accumulated honors for permitting defeat, he was sent to recover prestige by negotiating the Treaty of Shimoneseki. In 1896 he went as special Commissioner to attend the Coronation of the Emperor of Russia and has been suspected of throwing his weight unduly into the forwarding of Muscovite ambitions in the Orient. His return through Europe and the United States made him a great popular figure, and he arrived in China again to find himself at the height of his influence, living, as we have seen, just long enough afterwards to render services to the foreign population during the Boxer troubles.

Foreign Affairs. For several years after the conclusion of peace little or no change was apparent in China upon the surface. The Emperor exerted little or no influence and the humbled Dowager was apparently indifferent to the fate of Manchuria, from which Russia showed no signs of budging. In several other directions concern was given to the Chinese Government, notably in Tibet, where, in 1904, Great Britain felt herself obliged to interfere. The city of Lhassa was occupied by General Younghusband in August of that year, but in the end, after the flight of the Dalai Lama to Mongolia and the exaction of certain pledges the country was handed back to the suzerain power. The real question of the day was Manchuria. The protests of Japan, Great Britain and the United States against its continued occupation secured from Russia the promise to evacuate in eighteen months from April, 1902, but as there was manifested no intention of fulfilling the promise, Japan pushed the matter to the ordeal of war, and on Feb. 8, 1904, the conflict which had long been regarded as inevitable commenced.

RESULTS OF THE RUSSO-JAPANESE WAR. The war between Japan and Russia which was waged during 1904 and 1905 concerns China for two special reasons. First, it was fought for the most part on Chinese soil; secondly, the results affected China vitally. Directly, China was affected through the fact that Japan succeeded to the privileges of Russia in the Liao tung peninsula and in Manchuria. Korea also now came under the direct rule of Japan, though the formal annexation did not take place until 1910. More important still were the indirect results which showed themselves in a new spirit making powerfully for reform and a revived instinct of nationality. Army reform was carried out in several of the provinces, notably by the Viceroys Yuan Shih kai and Chang Chih tung.

THE AWAKENING OF CHINA.[4] Even the Empress Dowager was influenced by the new spirit. She had become much more conciliatory to foreigners since the dark days of 1900, and now set herself, cautiously and tentatively, to carry out some of the very reforms she had so ruthlessly cut off in 1908. In 1905 an Imperial Commission headed by Prince Tsai Tse, was appointed to study out a system of representative government with a view to granting Parliamentary control. The Commission in leaving Peking was greeted with a bomb which showed that the old spirit was by no means dead, but on its return edicts were issued promising at some time in the future a National Assembly. A further Edict in 1908 announced that a Parliament would be convoked nine years from that date.

OTHER REFORMS. A renewal of the anti-opium agitation at this time led to definite and far-reaching results. An edict was published September, 1906, ordering all opium-smoking to cease in ten years.[5] The opium dens of Peking were closed on the last day of 1906 and the coöperation of the Government of India was obtained to arrange for the annual decrease of exportation by 10 per cent. for four years, and subsequently, if it was shown that China was really in earnest, and was not taking advantage of the opportunity to increase its own production of the drug. The opium dens of Hongkong were closed in 1908 and everything that has since happened goes to show a sincere desire to bring an iniquitous traffic to an end. Meanwhile, educational reform was advancing steadily and a decree was issued in September, 1905, announcing that from the beginning of 1906 the old method of examination would cease. The old examination halls were in certain places abolished, temples were transformed into schoolhouses, primary schools for girls were established, thousands of students were sent abroad to Japan and elsewhere, and, as illustrating the desire of the authorities to emphasize moral teaching, Confucius was raised to the same rank as Heaven and Earth. "In thanking the throne for the honor conferred on his ancestors, the head of the family urged that at the new college founded at the birthplace of Confucius the teaching should include foreign languages, physical culture, political science and military drill." [6]

Death of the Emperor and the Empress Dowager. On November 14, 1908, according to the official account, the Emperor, whose health had manifestly suffered from his semi-incarceration, passed away. On the following day the last great representative of the spirit which had won China for the Manchus, the Dowager Empress Tsz hsi, followed her nephew to the shades of the ancestors. Rumors of a violent ending in either or both cases were not unnaturally rife, and in some instances circumstantial accounts were given of a great Palace tragedy, but the matter may perhaps best be left in obscurity undisturbed by speculation. One may be permitted to admire the high spirit of the dead Empress without condoning her crimes, and one may certainly be permitted to lament the ineffectuality of a character like that of Kwang hsu, genuinely disposed towards reform, yet condemned to beat helpless wings against the barriers imposed by circumstances, and by personalities stronger than his own. Perhaps his great mistake was an over-rash enthusiasm in 1898. Even on this point he may be permitted to make his own defense:—"I have been accused of being rash and precipitate, and of attempting great political changes without due consideration. This is an entire mistake. I have thought over the condition of my country with great seriousness for several years. Plan after plan has come before my mind, but each one I was afraid to put into action, lest I should make some blunder that would bring sorrow upon my Empire. In the meanwhile China is being dismembered. Shang tung has been occupied by the Germans. The Liao tung peninsula practically belongs to the Russians, and Formosa has been given over to the Japanese. Whilst I am waiting and considering, my country is falling into pieces, and now, when I attempt heroic measures I am accused of rashness. Shall I wait till China has slipped from my hands and I am left a crownless King?"

NOTES

1. A sane discussion of the Missionary Problem in China will be found in Chester Holcomb's *"The Real Chinese Question."*

2. For the Siege of the Legations and Boxer Revolt the following may be commended: *"China in Convulsion,"* A. H. Smith; *"Siege Days,"* A. H. Mateer; *"The Siege of Peking,"* W. A. P. Martin; *"China's Book of Martyrs,"* Luella Miner; *"The Outbreak in China,"* Dr. F. L. Hawks Pott. Also, from the point of view of one who visited Peking immediately after, Pierre Loti's *"Les Dernieres Jours de Pekin."*

3. The flight of the Emperor is described by Mr. Francis Nichols in *"In Hidden Shensi."*

4. Read *"The Awakening of China,"* by Dr. W. A. P. Martin.

5. For a strong indictment of the Opium traffic and a description of its results, read Samuel Merwin's *"Drugging a Nation."* Also Report of the Opium Commission, 1912.

6. Encyclopedia Britannica (11th Ed.) vi 211a.

CHAPTER XIII

THE REVOLUTION

A. D. 1911-1912.

*Accession of Hsuan tung—signs of the times—
the anti-dynastic movement—Sun Yat sen—the
revolution—Yuan Shih kai—peace negotiations—
abdication of the Emperor—end of the Manchu
dynasty.*

Kwang hsu was followed immediately by the
proclamation of the infant nephew of the late Emperor, *Pu Yi,* son of Prince Chun. The child
monarch received the title of Hsuan tung and his
father was appointed Regent, while the two great
Viceroys, Yuan Shih kai and Chang Chih tung,
were named as Grand Guardians of the Heir.
With another child upon the throne the outlook
was at least uncertain, but at this moment few
could have predicted the events so soon to rise
above the horizon.

Signs of the Times. An event of bad omen
shortly after the commencement of the new reign
was the dismissal of Yuan Shih kai, whose rheumatism was urged as an excuse for his compulsory
retirement, but who was probably feared on ac-

count of his foreign-trained troops. In other respects the tide of reform seemed still flowing. Railway developments were manifest on every hand. The Peking-Kalgan Railway was opened in October, 1909; the same year the line from Shanghai to Nanking was opened for through traffic; and in 1910 the French line was completed from Hanoi to Yunnan fu. Of still greater moment was the constitution of the Provincial Assemblies in 1909 and the creation of a Senate in the following year. Nevertheless, with all these signs of reform initiated by the government, deeper forces were at work, of which apparently the authorities were quite unaware.

The Anti-dynastic Movement. At the beginning of the Revolution which was so soon to come, a revolutionary agent is reported to have said: "Our party does not draw its force from its groups, but from exterior organizations, societies, corporations, associations of every kind. We launch forth our ideas; they fall where they can, always, however, on good soil. With us revolutions are made with the deep-seated forces of the race which, at a given moment, which we are unable to predict, manifest themselves abruptly." This is a truth which has not always been appreciated. Republicanism did not conquer in China by its own means, but by taking advantage of means provided by many different elements. Yet there was one man who at this time and for long before had been working to bring the various groups into harmony and to make possible the overthrow of the Manchu dynasty, and the establishment of a Chinese Republic.

Sun Yat sen. This man was Dr. Sun Yat sen,[1] who deserves to be remembered as much for the years that he spent in obscure and sometimes apparently hopeless agitation as for the achievements which brought his name prominently into the newspapers of the world. *Sun Wên*, or, as he is more generally called, Sun Yat sen, was born in 1866 in the province of Kwangtung, and at the age of thirteen accompanied his mother to Honolulu. Here for three years he was a pupil in the Anglican Mission School, Iolani College, and was then transferred to Oahu College. Returning to China, he entered Queen's College, Hongkong, and, after another visit to the Hawaiian Islands, took up the study of medicine at Canton. Subsequently he was at the College of Medicine in Hongkong, but soon commenced the career of an agitator and organizer against the Manchus. Forced to flee from China, he visited New York and London, where in 1896 he put forth what might be called the first manifesto of the Revolution. He declares that since the authorities at Peking had failed to learn the lesson which contact with the outside world had given them, he considered the door closed to pacific methods and would henceforth be an advocate of violence. He arrived in London on the first of October, 1896, and was kidnapped on the 11th, at the instance of the Chinese Government, as he says, "almost before he had learned to distinguish between Holborn and the Strand." Confined in the Chinese Legation, he made his imprisonment known to friends through a paper thrown into the street, and his liberation was promptly secured by the British Government. In the years that followed Dr. Sun labored indefatigably for his cause, traveling incessantly under all kinds of disguises, entering into relations with men and societies, obtaining money for his projects and writing in explanation of them. "The old monarchy must transform itself into a Republic," he wrote in 1904, and two years after, in Tokyo, he succeeded in welding together the different elements of the anti-dynastic movement, so as to give tangible purpose to the revolutionists of every color. How well he laid his plans the events of the fall of 1911 will bear witness.

THE REVOLUTION. There are some things which are so universally anticipated that when they do happen they take everybody by surprise. It was so with regard to the Chinese Revolution. Every newspaper, every missionary, every diplomat, foretold it time and time again. Yet when the outbreak came in September, 1911, the exclamation on the lips of all was "How sudden!" In a sense it was sudden, because the explosion did not take place at the contemplated time. A *coup de main* had been attempted as far back as 1907 on the frontier of Tongking and had failed. The insurrections broke out here and there, any one of which might have fired the main charge. In the summer of 1911 those in the secret knew it would come soon, but it came six months sooner than had been planned. The immediate cause was the Sze ch'uen Railway strike, due to the fear that the Four Power Loan would lead not only to the introduction of foreign capital and material, but also of foreign political control. The strike necessitated the movement of troops from Wu chang westward, and this movement led to the rising in Wuchang against the Manchus. Three ringleaders were promptly decapitated, but their blood was the seed out of which the Revolution sprang with magical force. With the Revolutionary Committee alive to its opportunity and Li Yuan hung at the head of the revolutionary army, in fifteen days all the lower Yang tsze kiang valley was lost to the Empire, and by mid-November fourteen provinces had declared their independence. City after city, including I chang, Chang sha, Kiu kiang, were captured in October, and before the end of the month a remarkable and grovelling edict in the name of the Emperor appeared, "a whining appeal for the mercy of the people," combined with a promise to grant a Constitution and remove the grievances of the insurrectionists. Shanghai went over to the rebels on November 1; Soo chow and Hang chow followed suit, and the warships under Admiral Sah went

YUAN SHIH KAI

over in a body. In an edict of November 4 the
Emperor is made to say: "Hereafter anything
which the people may suggest, if it is in accord-
ance with public opinion, we will openly adopt.
Heaven owns the people and provides rulers for
them. The people's ears and eyes are Heaven's
ears and eyes."

Yuan Shih kai. Meanwhile the authorities at
Peking were moved to call Yuan Shih kai from his
seclusion. He was the only man who seemed likely
to succeed; if he failed, the Grand Council would
not be sorry to witness his disgrace. He de-
murred somewhat, naturally doubtful as to
whether his "rheumatism" was sufficiently healed,
but eventually arrived at Peking on November 13,
accepted the Premiership, chose a cabinet, composed largely of unknown quantities, and prepared
to gain time by negotiations. With Nanking as
yet untaken and Wuchang and Han yang recap-
tured, it was evidently the psychological moment
for diplomacy. By securing a truce Yuan Shih
kai strengthened his position from day to day
and, though personally in favor of a limited
monarchy, was prepared to accept the real
mandate of the people for the creation of a Republic.

Peace Negotiations. The resignation of the
Regent on December 6 simplified matters, as he
had been vacillating throughout. In his place the
Empress Dowager was appointed. The Shanghai
Conference was held the third week of December,

Tang Shao yi representing the Imperialists and Wu Ting fang the Republicans. The Revolutionary Committee was even at this time urging the Presidency of the Republic upon Yuan Shih kai, but the astute Premier was still non-committal, and the Conference broke up without result two or three days after its opening. Nevertheless, the drift towards the Republic was plainly irresistible, and on December 28 the Imperial family left Peking, whilst an edict proclaimed that the question of Monarchy or Republic was to be left to a National Assembly. The next day a provisional Convention, meeting at Nanking, elected Dr. Sun Yat sen the first President of the Chinese Republic. In this capacity he held a review of the fleet at Shanghai on Jan. 12, 1912.

ABDICATION OF THE EMPEROR. Even without the help of the projected National Convention affairs were now shaping themselves towards a certain end. All through January, 1912, plans were being considered for the abdication of the Imperial house. These plans were favored by Prince Ching, who was convinced of the hopelessness of reëstablishing Manchu authority in the provinces. The Nanking Committee was perfectly willing to coöperate with Yuan Shih kai in this matter, and Sun Yat sen showed his customary reasonableness and unselfishness in his willingness to retire from the Presidency in favor of the elder statesman. However, the truculent opposition of the ex-Boxer leader, Tieh liang, delayed matters without assisting the cause of the Manchus, and it was not till February 7 that the announcement of the abdication of Hsuan tung was made. It secured suitable and generous provision for the Emperor, Princes and hereditary nobles, and declared that all "the Five Families," Chinese, Manchus, Mongols, Muhamadans and Tibetans should be treated on an equal footing.

END OF THE MANCHU DYNASTY. The two hundred and sixty-seven years of Manchu rule ended on February 12, 1912. On this day three edicts, each commencing in the customary way, were issued. The first runs in part as follows: "To-day the people of the whole Empire have their minds bent upon a Republic, the Southern provinces having initiated the movement and the northern generals having favored it subsequently. The will of Providence is clear and the people's wishes are plain. How could I for the sake of the glory and the honor of one family thwart the desire of teeming millions? Wherefore I (the Empress Dowager) with the Emperor decide that the form of Government in China shall be a Constitutional Republic to comfort the longing of all within the Empire and to act in harmony with the ancient sages, who regarded the throne as a public heritage." Yuan Shih kai is then given plenary power to establish a Provisional Republican Government and to act in coöperation with the Republican Provisional Government at Nanking to assure peace and tranquillity.

The third edict exhorts all to quietness and harmony and speaks of the desire of the Throne to terminate the period of anarchy and to restore to the land the blessings of peace.

Sun Yat sen at once sent a telegram expressing his extreme delight at the news of the Emperor's abdication, and requesting the presence of Yuan Shih kai at Nanking immediately. But the latter wisely enough declined to leave Peking, and ere long a remarkable deputation, representing New China, frock-coated and silk-hatted, arrived at the Capital to place in the hands of the new President the tremendous responsibility a successful revolution had entailed.

The End of a Dynasty.   The feelings of the world were perhaps most fittingly voiced in the words of a striking leading article which appeared in the London "*Times*," February 16, 1912:—

"The 'Son of Heaven' has abdicated, the Manchu dynasty reigns no longer, and the oldest Monarchy of the world has been formally constituted a Republic.   History has witnessed few such surprising revolutions and none perhaps of equal magnitude, which has been carried out in all its stages with so little bloodshed.   Whether the last of these stages has been reached is one of the secrets of the future.   Some of those who know China best cannot but doubt whether a form of Government so utterly alien to Oriental conceptions and to Oriental traditions as a Republic can be suddenly substituted for a Monarchy in a na-

tion of four hundred millions of men, whom kings
with semi-divine attributes have ruled since the
first dim twilight of history. China or, at all
events, articulate China has willed to have it so.
She has embarked with a light heart upon this
great adventure and we heartily desire that it
may bring her the progressive and stable government she craves."

NOTE

1.   The book *"Sun Yat Sen and the Awakening of China,"* by the Reformer's friend, Dr. James Cantlie, is disappointing and omits many important facts.

CHAPTER XIV

THE CHINESE REPUBLIC

The installation of Yuan Shih kai—administering the Republic—a year after—the Mongolian situation—financial affairs—the Anglo-Chinese Opium agreement—Death of the Empress Lung Yu—the electoral system—the opening of Parliament—a call to prayer—Conclusion.

INSTALLATION OF YUAN SHIH KAI. The formal installation of Yuan Shih kai as Provisional President took place at Peking on March 10. The ceremony is described as "stately and impressive and worthy of the historic occasion." The oath taken by Yuan runs as follows: "Since the Republic has been established many works have been performed. I shall endeavor faithfully to develop the Republic, to sweep away the disadvantages of absolute Monarchism, to observe the Constitutional laws, to increase the welfare of the country, and to cement together a strong nation, embracing all the five races. When the National Assembly appoints a permanent President I shall retire. This I swear before the Chinese Republic." On April 1 Dr. Sun Yat sen and the Provisional Government resigned the seals of office, the first elected President of the Republic retiring with the respect due to an unselfish and high-minded patriot. On April 29 an Advisory Council representing all the Provinces, Mongolia, Tibet and Koko nor, assembled at Peking under the presidency of Lin Sen, a relative of the famous Commissioner Lin of the Opium-war fame. A deeply impressive address was delivered by Yuan Shih kai and it was generally conceded that the outlook was hopeful.

ADMINISTERING THE REPUBLIC. Notwithstanding, however, a hopeful outlook the new President had in administering the Republic difficulties with which to contend which would have staggered a less experienced statesman. Some of these we shall have to speak of presently, but the result of Yuan's first few months of office was undoubtedly to strengthen his position in the country. The appointment of Dr. G. E. Morrison as Political Adviser brought to his side the assistance of one whose wide knowledge of foreign affairs and intimate acquaintance with existing conditions in China (arising from fifteen years' residence) were bound to be of the highest value. The Cabinet under Tang Shao yi was not a success, but a new Cabinet under Lu Cheng was nominated and approved by the Advisory Council in June. In August a somewhat troublesome question arose over the arrest and subsequent execution of General Chang Chin wu and General Hwang hui on the charge of promoting a second revolution in

the interest of some southern malcontents. There
was naturally a good deal of protest on the part
of radical sympathizers, but the President's strong
position was proved and no crisis came.

A YEAR AFTER. Apart from two difficulties
of a special character still to be described, the
outlook for the Republic a year after the Revolution was not discouraging. Writing a few weeks
before this, Dr. Morrison says: "People hardly
realize the immense change that has had to take
place in the administration of the country. Under the old *régime* no man could hold office in the
province of his birth. Now the reverse rule is
observed. Most officials in the provinces are now
natives of the provinces in which they are serv-
ing. Surely the interests of the province are
thus better served than under the old system. . . .
For the first time the people who pay the
taxes have a voice in the expenditure of their
taxes. These changes have involved the recasting
of the whole internal machinery of government.
That the change has been effected with such com-
parative smoothness should inspire hope in the
future of the country and should enable observers
to realize how little foundation there is for hys-
terical and sensational forecasts of civil war and
disruption." This was the situation when the
anniversary of the Revolution was observed October 10, 1912. There were certain political
changes and the inevitable readjustments following from the adaptation of the Chinese patriarchal

system to the conditions of western commercial life. Beyond this, the substance of the national existence remained the same. The London "*Times*" asserts on September 27: "All this will remain in spite of the change from the Manchu Dynasty to a so-called Republic. The heads of the Republic will merely take the paternal position of the Emperors to themselves and as likely as not will either disguisedly or openly perpetuate another dynasty. Indeed no other solution to a patriarchal country seems possible. This revolution, then, is not really an important change in China, it is not a social revolution, effecting a social change. It is only a change of directors. The main business will remain the same." On this point, of course, opinion will differ.

THE MONGOLIAN SITUATION. Two difficulties have been mentioned which it has been the fate of the Republican Government to encounter from the very start. The first is that relating to Mongolia. Soon after the beginning of the Revolution Mongolia declared its independence of China and established itself under an ecclesiastical ruler, known as the Hutukhtu. Under ordinary circumstances the new Republic could probably have overcome the insurrectionary movement and Mongolia could have been brought to occupy the position among the Five Families indicated by the new flag. But as time went on it became apparent that behind the Mongolian desire for independence was intrigue on the part of Russia. This intrigue culminated in a Treaty made directly between Russia and Mongolia without reference to the supreme claims of China. The text of the Treaty was as follows:

"1. The Imperial Russian Government shall lend Mongolia support in the maintenance of the autonomous *régime* established by the latter, and in vindication of her right to maintain a National Army and to prevent the invasion of her territory by Chinese troops or its colonization by Chinese subjects.

"2. The Regent of Mongolia and the Mongolian Government concede to Russian subjects and to Russian trade in Mongolian territory the enjoyment of the same rights and privileges as heretofore and as set forth in the annexed protocol. It is understood that subjects of other powers are not to receive in Mongolia more extensive rights than those conceded to Russians.

"3. If the Mongolian Government considers it to be necessary to conclude a special agreement with China or any other Foreign State such agreement is not to traverse or modify the articles of this Treaty and Protocol without the assent of the Imperial Russian Government."

This placed China in the difficult position of appearing to allow Mongolia to drift, unless she were prepared to make war, even to the extent of a conflict with Russia. In view of the financial situation this later course was plainly impossible.

Nor was this the worst. Encouraged by the apparently successful defection of Mongolia and probably influenced by the same subtle diplomacy, Tibet has practically taken the same attitude towards the Republic and both territories seem at the present time to have conspired to break up the unity of the Five Families.

FINANCIAL AFFAIRS. The great weakness, hitherto, of the Republic has been financial rather than political. In other words the political complications might have been overcome had the new Government had at its disposal money wherewith to discharge existing obligations and promote new enterprises. Soon after the birth of the Republic it was sought to make a loan of $300,000,000 through a group of bankers representing England, Germany, France, the United States, and afterwards Russia and Japan. This was known as the *Six Power Loan*. It was not popular in China where the cry was raised that the country was being mortgaged to the foreigner. Nor was it much liked by the foreign banks which had had sad experience of loans to such countries as Turkey, Persia, Morocco, and Honduras. An attempt was indeed made to raise the required sum by an internal national loan but, in the case of so poor a country as China, the idea was doomed to failure from its inception. Then came the attempts in the fall of 1912 to float a loan of $50,-000,000 in London, to be secured on the free surplus of the salt *gabelle*, and to be used for the repayment of existing loans and the Boxer indemnity. This was naturally opposed by the Six Power Group and also by the British Government. Nevertheless, the loan was floated in October and one half issued. But all attempts to reconcile the conflicting interests of prospective lenders proved abortive and by the end of 1912 China was financially in a very serious situation. She was in default on the indemnity; the Powers had not yet replied to the request for an extension of time; no advances had been arranged from the Crisp loan; moreover, France and Russia were working together and threatening to make China bankrupt. The danger of foreign intervention was never so near as at this time. Things have not greatly improved perhaps since. President Wilson made it clear in one of his earliest statements that so far as the American Government is concerned the Six Power Group is at an end. Smoother water, however, was reached with the re-election of Yuan Shih kai by the National Assembly.[1]

THE ANGLO-CHINESE OPIUM AGREEMENT. A difficulty of a lesser kind, yet still serious, lay in the doubt as to whether China was faithfully fulfilling her obligations to Great Britain in the reduction of the opium crop. It was reported that while in the ports the disposal of the imported opium had been to such an extent frustrated that there was an enormous accumulation of stock in the hands of the merchants, that a large opium crop had nevertheless been harvested throughout

China and that provinces which had previously re-duced their area of cultivation had again planted the poppy on a large scale. A warning was there-upon issued to the Chinese Government, which had some excuse for the reply that the disturbed state of the country during the Revolution and since had led to some districts disregarding the agree-ment but that the Peking authorities were ear-nestly endeavoring to comply with the provisions of the Treaty. In any case, we must recognize the great progress made by China in the campaign against the drug and the likelihood that an in-iquitous chapter in the history of commerce will be closed by 1917.

DEATH OF THE EMPRESS, LUNG YU. On Feb. 22, 1913, the Empress Dowager, Lung Yu, passed away, possibly from the effects of a dose of poison, but, according to the news given out, from an acute malady resembling appendicitis. She pos-sessed much of the grim and masterful character of her illustrious aunt and had always been un-sympathetic with the ideals and projected reforms of her husband, the Emperor Kwang hsu. In his last years she had played the part of a spy in the interest of Tsz hsi.

THE ELECTORAL SYSTEM. In the autumn of 1912 the promulgation of the Electoral laws di-rected the attention of the people of China to the fact that they were soon to take part in the elec-tion of delegates to the Senate, House of Repre-sentatives and Provincial Assemblies. The primaries were to be held in December, 1912, and the final elections in January. The new National Assembly was to be bi-cameral. The Senate was to consist of members elected by the Provincial Assemblies for a term of six years, ten senators to be returned by each Provincial Assembly twenty-seven by the Electoral colleges of Mongolia, eight by the Central Educational Society and six by Chinese residing abroad. One-third of the Senators will retire every two years and, to ensure this, the various groups will be divided by lot into three classes to serve respectively two, four and six years. The House of Representatives will be formed on a basis of proportionate representation, one representative to about eight hundred thousand people. The qualifications for voting are said to be not very exacting, yet on account of deficiency of education the number of voters at present is comparatively small. Those who have been deprived of civil rights, are bankrupts, opium smokers, insane or illiterate may neither vote nor be elected. Monks, priests, naval and military officers, judges and administrative officials generally are also deprived of these privileges.

The Opening of Parliament. Both houses of the new Parliament were opened on April 8. It is described as an impressive ceremony. "At 10 o'clock the joint inauguration of the Senate and the House of Representatives took place in the Lower Chamber, while simultaneously one hundred and one guns boomed outside the adjacent city wall. Within the House were assembled five hundred representatives out of a total membership of five hundred and ninety-six, and also a hundred and seventy-seven Senators out of two hundred and seventy-four. Nearly all wore frock coats, and appeared fully to realize the responsibility of their position. The public galleries were crowded almost to suffocation with Chinese and foreign visitors. At 11 o'clock the assembled bands played the National Anthem and the members stood up while the senior member of the House of Representatives, on behalf of both houses, formally declared Parliament open."

A Call to Prayer. That the momentousness of the situation was not unrealized by those in authority is shown by the remarkable message adopted by the Cabinet and telegraphed by the Chinese Government to the leaders of the Chinese Churches in China for transmission throughout the world. The text is as follows:

"Prayer is requested for the National Assembly, now in session, for the newly established Government, for the President yet to be elected, for the Constitution of the Republic, that the Government may be recognized by the Powers, that peace may reign within our country, that strong virtuous men may be elected to office, that the Government may be established upon a strong foundation. Upon receipt of this telegram you are requested to notify all churches in your province that April twenty-seventh has been set aside as a day of prayer for the nation. Let all take part." Probably the issuance of such an appeal is without precedent in the world's history. It ought to be of good omen for the future of the Republic.

CONCLUSION. The re-election of Yuan Shih kai, the acceptance by the Chinese Government of the Five Power Loan agreement on April 28th are both events which may be regarded as offering a reasonable guarantee of the stability of the new form of government. At this moment to say more might be rash.

The Emperor Kang hsi is said to have built the wonderful marble junk in the palace grounds of Peking with the belief that it would be in its perpetuity a symbol of the continuance of the Manchu dynasty. The question on the lips of all interested in the future of China must necessarily be, Will the Ship of the Republic endure? There are various views which may be chronicled without the writer venturing upon the risky *rôle* of the prophet. There are, first of all, the out and out pessimists. These believe that things have already gone so far that China's day is already over. Mongolia and Tibet, they say are already lost, and Manchuria as good as lost. China is sold to the money-kings of Europe and cannot even spend the money she borrows except for objects dictated by the powers. Russia and France have intrigued so that they hold China in their grasp, while Japan is an unwilling witness of Russia's gradual recovery of the ground she lost in 1905, and Great Britain grumblingly lets things go as they are going in Asia in order to maintain France's friendship in Europe. Yuan Shih kai is between the upper and nether mill-stones of Manchu hope of restoration and the southern desire for more radical reformation. That is one view.

Another is that of the extreme reformers, represented in the Kwo ming tang, men who dream dreams and see visions of a more thorough-going Republicanism than has yet been adventured. The party is powerful enough in the National Assembly and in the country to give plenty of trouble. Can they surmount all the practical difficulties in the way of translating their theories into action so as to supersede the present order?

Between the two extremes is the large body which recognizes in Yuan Shih kai the hope of China. "An opportunist of the Oriental type, guided by an extremely acute intelligence and sound judgment of his fellow-countrymen," he is still the man of the hour. He "leads the Republic, is the Republic, and draws the protagonists of the Revolution towards himself as if they were so many steel filings."

May we not see in the recent recognition of the Chinese Republic by the United States of America the expression of a belief on the part of a sympathetic America that the new government has come to stay and will triumphantly weather the present storms? There is much need not only for sympathy but also for practical help. As Lord

William Cecil puts it: "Let Western races join together to give them what they need, and in so doing they will not merely benefit China, though as China counts for a quarter of the population of this world, and is nearly equal to the number of men who have a right to call themselves civilized, that were no small merit; but they will do more, for they will by common acts of mercy and love bind each to each so that the horrid curse of racial hatred shall not be again able to divide them." [2]

Beyond all conflicting views we feel in the hearts of the millions of awakened Chinese and of those who sympathize with China's dream of a yet ampler destiny a hope which is inspired not merely by belief in the genius of this or that statesman, not merely by faith in this or that theory of political government, not merely by dependence upon this or that group of foreign powers but by earnest seeking after the way of truth and righteousness which enables nations as well as individuals to live long in the land. The words of the old Ode are still true—

"Good men are bulwarks; while the multitudes
  Are walls that ring the land;
  Great states are screens;
  Each family a buttress; the pursuit
  Of righteousness secures repose.

NOTES

1. A telegram dated Peking, May 14, is as follows: "The first advance of $1,200,000 was paid to-day to the Chinese government by representatives of the five-power group of financiers with whom China recently negotiated a loan for $125,000,000.

2. *"Changing China,"* p. 328.

ADDENDUM

That history is being made fast in China is
significantly shown by the fact that, since com-
pleting the above, enough has happened to provide material for an additional chapter or two.
A paragraph, however, must suffice. Some news
is good. It is good to hear of the favorable pros-
pects of the projected University for central
China for which funds may be provided out of the
Boxer Indemnity to Great Britain. It is good to
hear of the new interest on the part of Chinamen
in great works of development and engineering.
Less good is it to hear of Russia's success in de-
taching Mongolia from its former Chinese allegiance. The costly presents of the Czar just
received by the Hutukhtu should have recalled a
line from the Æneid about the Greeks who bring
gifts. It is still less good to hear of the efforts
on the part of the extreme Republicans of the
South to overthrow the government of Yuan Shih
kai and to promote the secession of the provinces of Kwang tung, Kiang si, Kiang su and Fuh
Kien. At the moment of writing (but who dare
venture upon prophecy?) the attempt seems
likely to fail. A new revolution would certainly
make powerfully for the partitioning of China

among the European powers and in any case must retard the proper progress of the Republic. A Chinese proverb says: "Heaven has not two suns, nor the people two kings." Times of divided rule have always been times of disaster. May there be in the present crisis patience and patriotism sufficient to lay securely the foundations for a more glorious epoch than Chinese history has yet been able to record!

APPENDIX

DYNASTIC TABLE

THE MANCHU DYNASTY A. D. 1644-1912

Shun chih	1644-1661
Kang hsi	1661-1722
Yung chêng	1722-1736
Kien lung	1736-1796
Kia king	1796-1820
Tao kwang	1820-1850
Hien fêng	1850-1860
Tung chih	1860-1875
Kwang hsu	1875-1908
Hsuan tung	1908-1912

NOTE—The Manchu chiefs associated with the conquest of China and the founding of the dynasty prior to Shun chih are as follows:

Tien ming (Nurhachu)	1616-1627
Tien tsung (Tsung têh)	1627-1644

INDEX